194
HIGH-IMPACT
LETTERS
for Busy
PRINCIPALS

Second Edition

194

HIGH-IMPACT
LETTERS
for Busy
PRINCIPALS

A Guide to Handling Difficult Correspondence

Second Edition

Marilyn L. Grady

CORWIN PRESS
A SAGE Publications Company
Thousand Oaks, California

For information:

Corwin Press
A Sage Publications Company
2455 Teller Road
Thousand Oaks, California 91320
www.corwinpress.com

Sage Publications Ltd.
1 Oliver's Yard
55 City Road
London EC1Y 1SP
United Kingdom

Sage Publications India Pvt. Ltd.
B-42, Panchsheel Enclave
Post Box 4109
New Delhi 110 017 India

Printed in the United States of America

Library of Congress Cataloging-in-Publication Data

Grady, Marilyn L.
194 high-impact letters for busy principals: A guide to handling
difficult correspondence / Marilyn L. Grady.—2nd ed.
       p. cm.
Rev. ed. of: 124 high-impact letters for busy principals.
ISBN 1-4129-1598-8 (cloth)
ISBN 1-4129-1599-6 (pbk.)
   1. School principals—Correspondence—Handbooks, manuals, etc.
2. Form letters—Handbooks, manuals, etc. I. Title: One ninty-four high-impact
letters for busy principals. II. Title: High-impact letters for busy principals.
III. Grady, Marilyn L. 194 high-impact letters for busy principals. IV. Title.
LB2831.9.G72 2006
651.7′52—dc22

                                                          2005037816

This book is printed on acid-free paper.

06 07 08 09 10 9 8 7 6 5 4 3 2 1

Acquisitions Editor:	Elizabeth Brenkus
Editorial Assistant:	Desirée Enayati
Copy Editor:	Colleen Brennan
Typesetter:	C&M Digitals (P) Ltd.
Cover Designer:	Lisa Miller

Contents

Acknowledgments

A special thanks to Kristy Carlson, Peggy Croy, Harriet Gould, Patrick Hunter-Pirtle, Barbara Marchese, and Kaye Peery for sharing their letter collections, resources, observations, and critiques of this volume. Elizabeth Grady and Jorge provided the spark, entertainment, patience, and good humor that inspired the completion of this book.

In addition, Corwin Press gratefully acknowledges the contributions of the following individuals:

Robert Denham, Interim Dean
School of Education, University of Redlands, Redlands, CA

Michelle Kocar, Principal
Heritage South Elementary School, Avon, OH

Ann Porter, Retired Elementary Principal
Grand Forks Public Schools, Grand Forks, ND

Gina Segobiano, Superintendent
Signal Hill School District # 181, Belleville, IL

Cathy West, Principal
Mountain Way Elementary School, Granite Falls, WA

About the Author

Marilyn L. Grady, PhD, is Professor of Educational Administration at the University of Nebraska-Lincoln (UNL). She is the author or coauthor of 16 books. Her research areas include leadership, the principalship, and superintendent-board relations. She has more than 175 publications to her credit.

She is the editor of the *Journal of Women in Educational Leadership.* Her editorial board service has included *Educational Administration Quarterly, The Rural Educator, The Journal of At-Risk Issues, The Journal of School Leadership, Advancing Women in Leadership On-Line Journal, Journal for Rural School and Community Renewal, International Journal of Learning,* and *The Journal for a Just and Caring Education.* She is the recipient of the Stanley Brzezinski Research Award and UNL's award for Outstanding Contributions to the Status of Women.

Grady coordinates an annual conference on women in educational leadership that attracts national attendance and is in its 20th year. She has served on the executive board of the National Council of Professors of Educational Administration, the Center for the Study of Small/Rural Schools, and Phi Delta Kappa Chapter 15. She is a member of the American Educational Research Association, the International Academy of Educational Leaders, the National Rural Education Association, the National Council of Professors of Educational Administration, Phi Delta Kappa, and the Horace Mann League.

She has been an administrator in K–12 schools as well as at the college and university levels. She received her BA in history from Saint Mary's College, Notre Dame, Indiana, and her PhD in educational administration with a specialty in leadership from The Ohio State University.

Introduction

Among the additions to this new edition of the book are parent education resource letters. Principals are called on to help with many parenting issues. These letters are designed to keep the communication channels open on issues that relate to student performance at school as well as health and wellness.

The number of positive, complimentary letters has been increased. There can never be too many complimentary letters. In fact, a principal's goal for each day may be to write at least one complimentary letter or note. Imagine the impact this small initiative could have in a school!

New letters are included that refer to achievement tests, assessments, standards, and the requirements of the No Child Left Behind Act. Also included are additional letters for behavior and crisis situations.

All of the letters in this edition have been reviewed and updated. The explosion of e-mail use since the first edition is noteworthy. Although many forms of communication can be handled as e-mail, there is no electronic substitute for the personal touch of a letter!

Mary Poppins's phrase, "well begun is half done," was the spirit guiding the preparation of this collection. The letters presented here and on the accompanying CD are intended as *templates*. They are meant to be a beginning. The templates have been designed to be generic, allowing the letter writers to *personalize them to specific situations*. Specialized language and educational jargon have been avoided so that the letters can be compatible with many different school settings.

The letters that can make a difference in the principalship are often the letters that principals have no time to prepare. Often, "must write" negative letters consume the principal's letter-writing energies. This collection of letters is primarily focused on the letters that principals have little or no time to prepare. Clearly, principals know how to write letters; they simply have incredible time constraints. The letters in this manual are not substitutes for the personalized letters that principals will craft. This collection is merely a starter kit.

The sequence of letters begins with the positives: thank-you letters, congratulations, best wishes, and other personal correspondence. These are the letters that build a culture of care throughout a school community. Recognition for a job well done or for a special contribution to the education of students are letters that make the work life of a school a positive experience. Remember: You can *never* write too many thank-you letters.

HIGH-IMPACT LETTERS FOR BUSY PRINCIPALS

Letters that are short, simple, and sincere can convey the right touch to the recipient. Letters that are personal, such as condolence notes, should be handwritten.

The letters are derived from a number of sources. Practicing principals contributed letters; these principals are cited in the acknowledgments. Other letters come from my files, from personal experiences as an administrator and teacher in elementary, junior high, and senior high school settings. Letters have also been collected during years of association with principals, with schools, and from parenting five children.

Some letters get written because they simply must be written. These may fall under a heading of discipline or problem behaviors, and they often have legal implications. School attorneys often assist in the preparation of these formal letters. This collection of letters is not designed to address these sensitive issues. Often, state statutes and specific school district policies frame these letters, and template letters would not be appropriate.

Principals provide many types of correspondence. Teacher appraisals, special education reports, forms pertaining to various uses, and newsletters are other types of written communication. This collection does not include these. School districts have teacher appraisal procedures and accompanying documentation based on district policies. For individuals who do not work in districts with established procedures, *The Marginal Teacher*[1] is an excellent resource. Special education procedures and correspondence deserve a special collection of letters targeted to the participants in this process. There are a number of companies that provide education forms for schools. School newsletters are an important communication device. Newsletter samples would fill an entire notebook, too. For these reasons, these forms of correspondence are not included in this collection.

These letters are for the principal leader who will be the key communicator for the school. They are meant to enhance and articulate the work of the schools and their leaders.

NOTE

1. *The Marginal Teacher: A Step-by-Step Guide to Fair Procedures for Identification and Dismissal* (3rd ed.), by C. E. Lawrence, was published in 2005 in Thousand Oaks, CA, by Corwin Press.

1

Thank-You Letters

Opportunities to say "thank you" abound. Yet the letters or notes do not get written. A principal who establishes a professional goal of crafting one thank-you note or letter per day will make great progress in establishing a positive climate for the principalship.

You can never write too many thank-you letters. Although the letters do not need to be long, they should be prompt, sincere, and personal. The occasions for thank-you letters or notes are seemingly endless:

Staff members who provide guidance to new teachers as mentors, who participate on interview teams, who assist students, or who serve on committees deserve a special note of thanks.

Students, too, must be thanked for their special help.

Parents need to be thanked for accompanying field trips, assisting with fundraisers, and serving on Parent-Teacher Associations.

Special guests of the school must be thanked for their contributions to the school program.

Speakers who make presentations may also be thanked for their positive influence on educational thinking.

Donors must certainly be thanked for their contributions.

Thank-You Letter 1.1

STAFF MENTOR

Elementary or Secondary

(Date)

(Name)

(Address)

Dear (Name):

Thank you for serving as a mentor to (Name) this year. Sharing your ideas and expertise about teaching has made this a rewarding and successful experience for (Name). Your understanding of learning theories, familiarity with school policies and procedures, teaching excellence, and interpersonal skills all contributed to a successful year. Your investment in the mentoring process affects the teaching profession as a whole as well as student learning.

Thank you for your contributions to the mentoring program.

Sincerely,

Principal

Thank-You Letter 1.2

STAFF TEAM MEMBER

Elementary or Secondary

(Date)

(Name)

(Address)

Dear (Name):

Thank you for your willingness to serve on the Teacher Interview Team. I really enjoyed the opportunity to work with you in the process of hiring new staff members. The task is critical, but with many hands, the work involved in screening applications, conducting phone interviews, and identifying the top candidates was a success. The new process we've used during our past two screenings has really assisted us in identifying those who best match the philosophy of (Name of School) School.

I hope that you found the process enjoyable. As always, change and revision help to improve our work. Please take a few minutes to reflect on the process and provide me with any ideas you might have for improving it.

Again, *thank you* for your contributions.

Sincerely,

Principal

Thank-You Letter 1.3

STAFF MEMBER LEAVING SCHOOL

Elementary or Secondary

(Date)

(Name)

(Address)

Dear (Name):

Thank you for your service to (Name of School) School. During your tenure here, you worked hard toward making (Name of School) School's mission come true. Your ability to work with students is exceptional. The "extras" you provided to assist student learning helped the entire team. We will all miss your humor too.

Please help us by completing the exit evaluation survey that you will receive from the personnel office. Your comments about your experiences at (Name of School) School will help us be the best we can be!

I wish you the best in your new job. You will be missed by all of us.

Sincerely,

Principal

Thank-You Letter 1.4

STAFF COMMITTEE MEMBER

Elementary or Secondary

(Date)

(Name)

(Address)

Dear (Name):

Thank you for agreeing to serve on the (Name of Committee) Committee. This is an important assignment, and your work on the committee will affect the entire school district.

The specific tasks for the committee are to

-
-
-
-

We will need to have the committee report by (date).

We look forward to hearing the results of your work.

Sincerely,

Principal

Thank-You Letter 1.5

STUDENT

Elementary or Secondary

(Date)

(Name)

(Address)

Dear (Student Name):

Thank you for your help with the (Activity) at (Name of School) School last week. You did a great job of organizing (Activity) and working with the younger students.

Although you volunteered for this assignment to meet your (Service Hours/Citizenship) requirement, you certainly displayed excellent interpersonal skills and the flexibility and knowledge to work with this age group. We would welcome your assistance with future activities.

On behalf of everyone who participated in (Activity), thanks!

Sincerely,

Principal

Thank-You Letter 1.6

PARENT(S), FIELD TRIP

Elementary

(Date)

(Name)

(Address)

Dear (Name):

Thank you for accompanying the (Class) class on their field trip to (Place). The students have made many comments about what a fantastic time they had. They particularly appreciated your great sense of humor.

Field trips are a wonderful educational experience for students. These events create lasting memories for the students. They provide hands-on learning opportunities that cannot be duplicated in the classroom. Without your help, this student trip would not have been possible.

So on behalf of the students, thanks so much.

Sincerely,

Principal

Thank-You Letter 1.7

PARENT(S), FUNDRAISING

Elementary

(Date)

(Name)

(Address)

Dear (Name):

Thank you for your assistance with our recent (Event) fundraising event. Your efforts resulted in profits of (Dollar Amount) for (Name of School) that exceeded our goals for the event. These funds will be used to (Fund's Uses).

Successful fundraising activities take time and organization. The success of the (Event) is clear evidence of your outstanding work.

As you know, the students at (Name of School) realize the benefits of the fundraising activities. On their behalf, thank you for your work.

Sincerely,

Principal

Thank-You Letter 1.8

PARENT(S), PTO/PTA

Elementary

(Date)

(Name)

(Address)

Dear (Name):

Thank you for your service as PTO/PTA (Position) during the (Year) school year. This work is very important to the experiences our children have at (Name of School) School. Your contributions provide the "something extra special" for the students.

Your work this year has resulted in some real successes. These include (Description of Successes). The number of parents who were involved in activities this year is truly remarkable.

The true beneficiaries of your efforts are the students at (Name of School) School.

Again, thank you for your efforts.

Sincerely,

Principal

Thank-You Letter 1.9

GUEST SPEAKER(S) (1)

Elementary

(Date)

(Name)

(Address)

Dear (Name):

Thank you for giving your valuable time and sharing an important message with our students. It was an excellent presentation.

I also appreciate the involvement of (Names) and their important messages to the students. Their participation provided great role models for the students. Please extend our thanks to (Names).

There were many positive comments about the quality of your presentations.

Thanks for helping make (Description) Week a success.

Sincerely,

Principal

Thank-You Letter 1.10

GUEST SPEAKER(S) (2)

Elementary or Secondary

(Date)

(Name)

(Address)

Dear (Name):

Thank you for the program you provided for our students. Although we strive to provide the best instructional experiences we can for our students, we cannot replicate the world of work experiences you presented to the students. I am sure they will remember your presentation and that it will be a source of inspiration as they pursue their occupational interests. Your contributions are greatly appreciated!

Sincerely,

Principal

Thank-You Letter 1.11

CONFERENCE SPEAKER

Elementary or Secondary

(Date)

(Name)

(Address)

Dear (Name):

I really enjoyed your presentation at the (Name of Conference) Conference. I was particularly interested in what you said about (Description). Your topic is particularly timely given the national emphasis on standards and assessments. I am sorry that all of our teachers were not able to attend the presentation.

Thank you for sharing your work in this area. It is really of critical importance to educators.

Sincerely,

Principal

Thank-You Letter 1.12

DONATION, GENERAL

Elementary or Secondary

(Date)

(Name)

(Address)

Dear (Name):

On behalf of the students at (Name of School) School, thank you for your generous contribution. The students at (Name of School) School will benefit from your contribution both now and in the future. In times of limited resources, contributions such as yours make an incredible difference in what's available to our students.

As a continuing reminder of your generosity, your name will be added to our Donor Honor Wall in the (Location) hall. We would like to have a special ceremony to recognize your contribution, and we will contact you soon to schedule this event. Your gift will truly be remembered at (Name of School) School!

Sincerely,

Principal

Thank-You Letter 1.13

DONATION, IN KIND

Elementary or Secondary

(Date)

(Name)

(Address)

Dear (Name):

On behalf of the students of (Name of School) School, I want to thank you for the donation of (Description) to our (Description) program.

Thank you for the support that (Name of Business) has shown (Name of School) School. The partnership with (Name of Business) has been a great association for the students and faculty. We value your assistance and association with our school.

Sincerely,

Principal

Thank-You Letter 1.14

DONATION, MONEY

Elementary or Secondary

(Date)

(Name)

(Address)

Dear (Name):

Please accept this as a receipt for your generous donation to the (Description). Your donation to the (Name of School) during (Year) totaled (Dollar Amount).

We appreciate your recognition of the needs of the students and the school. Without your support, we would be limited in the opportunities we are able to provide.

Thank you for your generous support.

Sincerely,

Principal

2

Appreciation Letters

Like thank-you letters, letters of appreciation should be written often. Many individuals deserve notes of appreciation as recognition for their efforts and the work they accomplish. Sometimes, we overlook opportunities to note these accomplishments because the work is "expected." However, principals can build a positive culture by acknowledging the "positives" in a school environment. Shifting the emphasis to what works and what's best in a school can build positive regard for all members of the school community. Individuals might receive appreciation letters for the following activities:

Staff members working with students during a special appreciation week or driving a bus deserve special notes of appreciation.

Volunteers who contribute their time and talent to a school deserve recognition and appreciation for their efforts.

Business partners provide opportunities for students and needed resources for schools. There are many opportunities to recognize the roles business partners play for students and schools through letters of appreciation.

Appreciation Letter 2.1

STAFF, GENERAL

Elementary or Secondary

(Date)

(Name)

(Address)

Dear (Name):

Thank you for working with (Name). We have been able to see the positive outcomes of your work with (Name). We really appreciate your efforts in (Description of Efforts). You are truly an asset to our school in the skills you bring to the educational enterprise.

Sincerely,

Principal

Appreciation Letter 2.2

STAFF, APPRECIATION WEEK

Elementary or Secondary

(Date)

(Name)

(Address)

Dear (Name):

Since this is a special week, I would like to take the opportunity to thank you for your fine work throughout the year. You are especially recognized for your (Description of Abilities). We regularly receive reports from students and parents about your positive impact on student learning.

Your work on behalf of our students really makes a difference. Thank you for your dedication and efforts.

Sincerely,

Principal

Appreciation Letter 2.3

STAFF, ROLE

Elementary or Secondary

(Date)

(Name)

(Address)

Dear (Name):

Thank you for your contributions to our staff and students in your role as a (Position). Your responsiveness to the many situations that have occurred at school has been exceptional. The staff and I appreciate your hard work and dedication.

The week of (Dates) is set aside as (Position) Appreciation Week. On (Day of Week), a special breakfast will be held to honor (Position). On (Day of the Week) from (Time) to (Time), the staff will host a special luncheon for (Position) in the cafeteria.

We look forward to sharing this special week with you.

Sincerely,

Principal

Appreciation Letter 2.4

STAFF DRIVER

Elementary

(Date)

(Name)

(Address)

Dear (Name):

Thank you for being an important part of (Name of School) School. We certainly recognize that driving a school bus is not an easy job. Keeping students seated and quiet while driving safely is serious work.

To recognize your contributions, we have set aside (Date) as Bus Driver Appreciation Day. On that day, from (Time) to (Time) A.M., we will have coffee and refreshments for our bus drivers in the school cafeteria. We look forward to sharing this special day with you.

Sincerely,

Principal

Appreciation Letter 2.5

VOLUNTEER

Elementary or Secondary

(Date)

(Name)

(Address)

Dear (Name):

Thank you for your many contributions to (Name of School). Please accept the enclosed Certificate of Appreciation for volunteering in the (Description). The students and teachers certainly appreciate your assistance.

We will have a special reception for our volunteers on (Date) at (Time) in (Location). We hope you will be able to join us for this special recognition.

We also hope you will continue to be involved with school activities!

Sincerely,

Principal

Enclosure:

Appreciation Letter 2.6

BUSINESS PARTNER

Elementary or Secondary

(Date)

(Name)

(Company Name)

(Address)

Dear (Name):

(Name of School) School is fortunate to have (Name of Business) as our school's business partner. We appreciate the many ways you have assisted the students and the school. Your presence in the classrooms and the mentoring of students has been particularly helpful.

Visiting your workplace was a memorable experience for the students. Not only did the students enjoy seeing (Business) but they returned to school more excited about the "world of work."

I hope this partnership will last for many years!

Sincerely,

Principal

Appreciation Letter 2.7

BUSINESS PARTNER, INVITATION

Elementary

(Date)

(Name)

(Company Name)

(Address)

Dear (Name):

On (Day of the Week), (Date), the (Students) of (Name of School) are sponsoring a (Event) in the cafeteria from (Time) to (Time). This (Event) will benefit the clubs and activities at (Name of School) School.

In appreciation for all that (Name of Business) does for (Name of School), we are enclosing two complimentary tickets for you and a guest to join us at the (Event). We hope to see you soon!

Sincerely,

Principal

3

Congratulations Letters

Many life events, as well as personal and professional accomplishments, deserve a personal note of congratulations. Often, these events slip by unnoticed or unheralded by principals. These events provide excellent opportunities for principals to extend recognition to those associated with the school. Building goodwill and a culture of accomplishment should be important goals for a principal.

Teachers might be congratulated for exhibitions of student work, receiving awards, being elected to office, completing advanced degrees, the birth of a child, adoptions, promotions, or student performance.

Parents might be congratulated for their child's receipt of an award, accomplishments, recognition in the newspaper, receipt of a scholarship, or winning a contest.

Students might be recognized for winning awards, receiving honors, or being "Stars of the Week."

Though not strictly letters, *news releases* might be used in conjunction with awards activities as a means of public congratulations.

Teams might be congratulated for winning awards or for their performances in state tournaments.

A *coach* might be congratulated for being selected Coach of the Year.

Individuals who choose to retire might also be congratulated for this life change.

Congratulations Letter 3.1

TEACHER, STUDENT WORK DISPLAY

Elementary or Secondary

(Date)

(Name)

(Address)

Dear (Name):

Congratulations on the outstanding exhibition of student (Description) work at the (Event). It was an excellent display. The range and variety of work was impressive. The number of students who had their work represented was noteworthy too. I'm certain that the students, their parents, and the community members enjoyed the display.

Thank you for making the exhibition possible.

Sincerely,

Principal

Congratulations Letter 3.2

TEACHER, AWARD

Elementary or Secondary

(Date)

(Name)

(Address)

Dear (Name):

Congratulations on winning the (Name of Award) Award. We realize that this award is given to only one educator in the nation each year. Because of your outstanding contributions to the field of (Subject) education, you were selected from all the applicants.

Your teaching talents are clearly recognized by all who have had the chance to work with you. The letters submitted in support of your nomination attest to this recognition. You certainly deserve this national honor.

It is a pleasure to have you as a teacher at (Name of School) School.

Sincerely,

Principal

Congratulations Letter 3.3

TEACHER, ELECTION TO OFFICE

Elementary or Secondary

(Date)

(Name)

(Address)

Dear (Name):

Congratulations on your election to the (Description). The large number of individuals who voted for you suggest the respect you have earned from your colleagues. You should be very proud of the outcomes of the election. We look forward to your leadership in this new position. If I can assist you in any way, please let me know.

Sincerely,

Principal

Congratulations Letter 3.4

TEACHER, DEGREE

Elementary or Secondary

(Date)

(Name)

(Address)

Dear (Name):

Congratulations on completing your master's degree. This is a truly noteworthy accomplishment. I know that the program you completed is quite rigorous. The great thing about an academic degree is that you never stop using it!

Congratulations on your achievement.

Sincerely,

Principal

Congratulations Letter 3.5

TEACHER OR STAFF, BIRTH OF CHILD

Elementary or Secondary

(Date)

(Name)

(Address)

Dear (Name):

Congratulations on the birth of your (Son/Daughter), (Name). We understand that (his/her) arrival was quite exciting. (He/She) will undoubtedly be a spectacular addition to your household. We look forward to meeting (Him/Her) soon.

Sincerely,

Principal

Congratulations Letter 3.6

TEACHER, PROMOTION

Elementary or Secondary

(Date)

(Name)

(Address)

Dear (Name):

Congratulations on your promotion to (Position) at (Name of School) School. This is a great tribute to your ability. I know you will do an excellent job.

Your leadership and organizational skills will serve you well in this new position. Your ability to get along with staff, students, and parents will also be an asset. Best wishes in your new position!

Sincerely,

Principal

Congratulations Letter 3.7

TEACHER, STUDENT ACHIEVEMENT

Elementary or Secondary

(Date)

(Name)

(Address)

Dear (Name):

Congratulations to you and your students on the students' recent performance on their (Name) tests. I know that you and the students worked very hard to improve the scores in (Subject) and (Subject). This is a major academic accomplishment.

Congratulations on the super effort!

Sincerely,

Principal

Congratulations Letter 3.8

PARENT(S) OR FAMILY OF
TEACHER, TEACHER'S AWARD

Elementary or Secondary

(Date)

(Name)

(Address)

Dear (Name):

I am pleased to inform you that (Teacher's Name) has been awarded the (Name of Award) for the (Year) school year. The (Name of Award) will be presented on (Date) at (Time).

(Name) truly deserves this award. (He/She) is an excellent teacher who always keeps students' needs foremost in (His/Her) efforts.

I would like you to attend the award ceremony that will be held in conjunction with the annual (Name of Conference) on (Day), (Date), at (Time) at the (Name of Room at Conference) in (City).

Congratulations on (Name's) accomplishments. Please call me if you have any questions about the event.

Sincerely,

Principal

Congratulations Letter 3.9

PARENT(S), STUDENT AWARD

Secondary

(Date)

(Name)

(Address)

Dear (Name):

Congratulations! (Name of student) has won the most-improved-student award for (Year). (Name of Student)'s grade point average increased from (GPA) to (GPA). Also, (Name of Student) had perfect attendance, was on time for every class, and had no disciplinary referrals during (Year). (Name of student) is making great progress at (Name of School) School. As a reward for (Name of Student)'s achievement, (He/She) will receive (Reward).

We recognize that you played a major role in (Name of Student)'s success, and we appreciate your assistance.

Sincerely,

Principal

Congratulations Letter 3.10

PARENT(S), STUDENT GPA

Secondary

(Date)

(Name)

(Address)

Dear (Name):

We are very pleased that your (Son/Daughter), (Name of Student), achieved a perfect 4.0 grade point average during the (Year) school year.

(Name of Student)'s name will be displayed on the special "4.0" plaque in the (Room of the School). We hope you will stop by to see it.

(Name of Student)'s hard work and your support are greatly appreciated.

Sincerely,

Principal

Congratulations Letter 3.11

PARENT(S), STUDENT MENTION IN NEWS

Elementary or Secondary

(Date)

(Name)

(Address)

Dear (Name):

Enclosed is a copy of the article about your (Son/Daughter), (Name), that appeared in the (Name of the Newspaper). Also enclosed is a copy of the photo that accompanied the article. We thought you might like to have an extra copy. This newspaper coverage is a fine tribute to (Name of Student)'s accomplishments. You must be very proud of (Him/Her)!

Sincerely,

Principal

Congratulations Letter 3.12

PARENT(S), STUDENT SCHOLARSHIP

Secondary

(Date)

(Name)

(Address)

Dear (Name):

Great news! The (Name of Business Company) has awarded your (Son/Daughter), (Name of Student), a (Name of Scholarship) scholarship for graduating with a (GPA) grade point average and for having four years of perfect attendance in high school. I know that you are proud of (Student's Name) accomplishments.

Congratulations and best wishes for (Student Name's) continued success!

Sincerely,

Principal

Congratulations Letter 3.13

PARENT(S), STUDENT CONTEST WINNER

Elementary or Secondary

(Date)

(Name)

(Address)

Dear (Name):

We understand that (Name of Student) recently won the (Name) Contest. This is a wonderful accomplishment since more than (Number) students from throughout the United States entered the contest.

(Name of Student)'s selection is certainly a reflection of (His/Her) accomplishments as a (Description). Congratulations to you and your (Son/Daughter)!

Sincerely,

Principal

Congratulations Letter 3.14

STUDENT, AWARD WINNER (1)

Elementary or Secondary

(Date)

(Name)

(Address)

Dear (Name):

Congratulations! You are the winner of the (Name of Award) Award. Among the accomplishments that contributed to your selection for this award were (Accomplishments). You certainly deserve this honor!

The award will be presented during the Annual (School Name) Award Ceremony on (Date) at (Time) in the (Location). Please be sure to share this information with your family and friends. We look forward to this special event.

Sincerely,

Principal

Congratulations Letter 3.15

STUDENT, AWARD WINNER (2)

Elementary or Secondary

(Date)

(Name)

(Address)

Dear (Name):

Congratulations on winning the (Name of Award). Your fine work is reflected in this achievement. This is a truly remarkable accomplishment. We received a number of fine compliments about you. These include (compliments).

We are proud that you represented our school so well. Congratulations on a job well done!

Sincerely,

Principal

Congratulations Letter 3.16

STUDENT, AWARD RECIPIENT

Elementary or Secondary

(Date)

(Name)

(Address)

Dear (Name):

We are extremely pleased that you are the recipient of the (Name of Award) Award. You were selected for this honor from a group of (Number) entries from the entire state of (Name of State). The judges' comments included the following remarks (Judges' Remarks). You should be particularly proud of your achievement.

We wish you continued success!

Sincerely,

Principal

Congratulations Letter 3.17

STUDENT, HONOR AWARD

Elementary or Secondary

(Date)

(Name)

(Address)

Dear (Name):

Congratulations on receiving the (Name of Honor) Honor for your quick response during the (Emergency). We are fortunate to have you as a member of our school community. You have displayed excellent citizenship characteristics as well as good judgment and decision making. Your initiative and action in that situation certainly deserve special recognition.

Well done (Student Name)!

Sincerely,

Principal

Congratulations Letter 3.18

STUDENT, STAR OF THE WEEK

Elementary or Secondary

(Date)

(Name)

(Address)

Dear (Name):

Congratulations on being selected as *Star of the Week*. I hope you enjoy this opportunity to share your special interests with the students and staff. I especially look forward to seeing your photo display and listening to your special presentation on (Date) at (Time) and in (Location). Remember to invite your family to join us for your special presentation.

I hope your week is great!

Sincerely,

Principal

Congratulations Letter 3.19

NEWS RELEASE

Secondary

(Date)

(Name)

(Address)

For Immediate Release

(Name of School) is to present (Name of Award) awards to students on (Date). (Name) will present the awards for outstanding (Name of Awards) to (Number) students at (Time), (Date), in Room (Room Number) of the (Name of Building) building.

Award recipients are (Name), (Name of School) High School; (Name), (Name of School) High School; and (Name), (Name of School) High School. These honorees were selected based on their exceptional (Accomplishments). The students' contributions ranged from (Contributions) to (Contributions).

A reception will follow the award ceremony. The award ceremony and reception are free and open to the public. For information, call (Phone Number) or e-mail (Name) at (e-mail address).

Congratulations Letter 3.20

TEACHER OR COACH, TEAM AWARD (1)

Elementary or Secondary

(Date)

(Name)

(Address)

Dear (Name):

Congratulations on winning the (Name of Award). You and the (Name of Team) Team have truly earned the prize. I know how hard you and the team worked to achieve this honor.

The trophy for winning the (Award) contest will be on display in Room (Room Number) of (Name of School) School.

Thank you for your efforts on behalf of the students.

Sincerely,

Principal

Congratulations Letter 3.21

TEACHER OR COACH, TEAM AWARD (2)

Secondary

(Date)

(Name)

(Address)

Dear (Name):

Congratulations to you and the (Name of Team) Team on winning first place in the State Tournament. The hard work, dedication, and extra effort certainly paid off.

It appeared that you faced some fine teams in the tournament matches. You should be extremely proud of the skills displayed by the athletes.

Congratulations on this major accomplishment!

Sincerely,

Principal

Congratulations Letter 3.22

COACH AWARD

Secondary

(Date)

(Name)

(Address)

Dear (Name):

Congratulations on being selected High School Football Coach of the Year. I know our staff, students, parents, and the community are proud that you have been selected.

Your hard work, dedication, leadership, and football expertise have been recognized both locally and at the state level. We have been extremely fortunate to have you as a football coach at (Name of School) High School for the past (number) years.

Congratulations on winning this award!

Sincerely,

Principal

Congratulations Letter 3.23

TEACHER, RETIREMENT

Elementary or Secondary

(Date)

(Name)

(Address)

Dear (Name):

Best wishes on your retirement from (Name of School) School. It is hard to imagine that you are retiring from teaching. You have been such an important part of this school and such a great influence on the lives of our students.

It has always been a pleasure to work with you. You will be greatly missed!

Best wishes as you enjoy your retirement.

Sincerely,

Principal

Congratulations Letter 3.24

STAFF, RETIREMENT

Elementary or Secondary

(Date)

(Name)

(Address)

Dear (Name):

Best wishes on your retirement and thank you for your many contributions to (Name of School) School.

It has been an honor and a pleasure to work with you.

I know the staff and students at (Name of School) School will miss you. You have left behind a fine legacy.

I hope your retirement years will be filled with great happiness. Best wishes to you!

Sincerely,

Principal

Congratulations Letter 3.25

STUDENT(S), NATIONAL MERIT SEMIFINALIST

Secondary

(Date)

(Name)

(Address)

Dear (Student Name):

Congratulations on your achievement in being selected as a National Merit Semifinalist. You should be especially proud of this accomplishment.

The teachers and administrators are extremely pleased with the recognition you have received for your accomplishment.

Good luck with the rest of your school year!

Sincerely,

Principal

Congratulations Letter 3.26

STUDENT(S), ALL-STATE BAND

Secondary

(Date)

(Name)

(Address)

Dear (Student Name):

Congratulations on being selected to the All-State Band. This accomplishment reflects on your efforts throughout the year.

We are all pleased that you have been chosen for this honor.

Sincerely,

Principal

4

Sympathy Letters

Letters of sympathy may be the most difficult of all letters to write. The writer is challenged to find appropriate words of comfort. The recipient is often inconsolable. The essential element of the sympathy letter is to say you are sorry for the loss or sadness of a friend or colleague; two examples follow. Simple, direct, and sincere are important guidelines for the expression of sympathy. Sympathy letters are *handwritten.*

Remembering the great qualities or special times with a deceased individual may be thoughtful additions to a sympathy letter. Depending on your relationship, flowers, memorials, or Mass cards may be appropriate tributes in addition to the sympathy note or card.

Deaths require the expression of sympathy through personal letters and notes.

Sympathy Letter 4.1

SYMPATHY LETTER (1)

Elementary or Secondary

(Date)

Dear (Name):

I was deeply saddened to learn of (Name)'s death. (Name)'s death is a sad loss for you and for (Name)'s friends at (Name of School) School. There really are no words to express this sadness.

Enclosed you will find cards and notes from the faculty, staff, and students. As you can see, the loss of (Name) has touched so many of us.

Our thoughts are with you.

Sincerely,

Sympathy Letter 4.2

SYMPATHY LETTER (2)

Elementary or Secondary

(Date)

Dear (Name):

We were very sorry to hear about (Name)'s death. The students and staff of (Name of School) extend our deepest sympathy to you on the death of (Name).

Because (Name) had such a great impact at the school, we have established a special award in (Name)'s name. This award will be given annually to an individual who reflects the ideals (Name) represented.

You know that you are in our thoughts.

Sincerely,

5

Get-Well Letters

Illness, operations, and accidents are events requiring acknowledgment. The spirit of the notes or letters should be one of care and concern. Reminding individuals that they are in your thoughts is the essence of the message. Occasions for get-well letters include the following:

Accidents are occasions that require notes of sadness and concern for the individual or the family of the individual.

Surgery and illness are events that require a letter or note of concern for the individual or the family.

Get-Well Letter 5.1

ACCIDENT

Elementary or Secondary

(Date)

Dear (Name):

We were all sorry to hear the news about your accident. (Name) called to tell us that you had (Description).

We hope that you will not have to stay too long in the hospital. (Name) indicated that you would be going to physical therapy after you are released from the hospital. If you need transportation assistance for those trips, we would like to help.

We look forward to your recovery and your return to school. You will be missed!

Sincerely,

Get-Well Letter 5.2

SURGERY

Elementary or Secondary

(Date)

Dear (Name):

We are pleased to hear that your surgery was successful. (Name) told us that you will be in the hospital for (Number) days and that the doctors believe that you should be home by (Date).

Your friends from school have arranged a schedule for visiting you and bringing meals for you and your family. We are all anxious to see you.

We miss you at (Name of School) School and look forward to your return.

Sincerely,

Get-Well Letter 5.3

TEACHER, SURGERY

Elementary or Secondary

(Date)

Dear (Teacher's Name):

It was wonderful news to hear that your surgery is over and you will be coming home soon. I hope that your recovery is swift.

Please do not be concerned about your work at school. Because you made such careful plans before your surgery, it has been easy to continue to make progress following the plans you provided.

All we are missing is YOU!

We look forward to seeing you soon!

Sincerely,

Get-Well Letter 5.4

FAMILY ILLNESS

Elementary or Secondary

(Date)

Dear (Name):

I am sorry to learn that (Name) is in the hospital. This must be a very difficult time for you and your family. I sincerely hope that (Name) will make a complete recovery.

The faculty and staff have contributed to the purchase of the enclosed gift cards for you and your family. If we can help in any way, please call me at (Telephone Number) or send me an e-mail (E-mail Address).

Sincerely,

6

Welcome
Letters

Welcome letters can set the tone for a school. These letters provide a positive dimension to new experiences, new programs, and meeting new people. A written welcome can ease a transition and provide information that makes the new situation less stressful and less intimidating. These letters are the extras that help make schools welcoming places. The following welcome letters might be sent:

Students might be welcomed to school at the beginning of a new school year.

Parents might be welcomed to a new school year. Parent welcome letters often include important information about the start of the school year, such as announcements of Open House dates and times. New faculty members may also be introduced to parents in the letter.

Neighbors of the school may deserve a "welcome to the school year" letter. This letter provides a bridge to positive neighborhood cooperation.

Staff welcome-back letters help set a positive tone for a new school year. They can also provide important school opening information. Staff letters can be used to introduce new staff members and also to greet new members of the school team. "Welcome-back" letters to staff should convey enthusiasm for a new school year and positive regard for the staff.

Welcome Letter 6.1

STUDENT

Elementary

(Date)

(Name)

(Address)

Dear (Student Name):

Welcome to (Grade) grade! I'm looking forward to the start of the school year and I hope you are too! You'll have a great time in (Teacher's Name) class. We have some special "welcome back" activities planned for the first week of school that I'm sure you'll enjoy. These activities include (List Activities).

See you next week!

Sincerely,

Principal

Welcome Letter 6.2

PARENT(S) (1)

Elementary

(Date)

(Name)

(Address)

Dear (Name):

Welcome to (Name of School) School. All of us at (Name of School) are anticipating another exciting year.

Joining the (Name of School) this year are (Names of New Faculty), (Subjects), (Grades).

First Day

The first day of school is (Date).

School Hours

School hours effective (Date):

8:55 A.M.–3:30 P.M. for all kindergarten through Grade 6 students.

Attendance and Tardiness

When absences or tardiness occurs, parents should notify the school office by calling (Phone Number) by (Time).

Lunches

School lunches will cost (Dollar Amount) per day. We use a computerized system to facilitate meal purchases. Please send your check for school meals to (Name) at (Address) by (Date). You will be required to keep track of the positive balance in the account so that your children are able to purchase meals. If you prefer, you can bring a check to school. Children may bring a cold lunch and purchase a carton of milk for (Amount) if they desire.

Please refer to the information in the packet regarding free and reduced lunch and breakfast qualifications.

If you have any questions about any of this information, please contact me at (Telephone Number) or at (E-mail Address).

We look forward to a great school year!

Sincerely,

Principal

Welcome Letter 6.3

PARENT(S) (2)

Secondary

(Date)

(Name)

(Address)

Dear (Name):

Welcome to (Name of School) School. We are looking forward to another great year! Because you may have questions about the start of the school year, the following information is provided for your assistance:

First Day of School	(Day of Week), (Date)
School Times	School starts at (Time) A.M. and ends at (Time) P.M.
Lunch	Students may purchase a school lunch for (Dollar Amount) or may bring a bag lunch. Students should deposit money in the computerized banking system to pay for their lunches. Reduced-fee or no-fee school lunches are also available. Information concerning reduced-fee or no-fee lunches is attached to this letter.
Locker Assignment	Locker assignments may be picked up in (Room Number) on (Date) from (Time) to (Time).
Class Schedules	Class schedules may be picked up in (Room Number) on (Date) from (Time) to (Time).
Supplies	Teachers will distribute supply lists.

Also included with this letter is a list of telephone numbers, e-mail addresses, and dates of upcoming events.

We hope the enclosed materials are helpful to you.

Sincerely,

Principal

Enclosures:

Welcome Letter 6.4

PARENT(S), INFORMATION SHEET

Secondary

Listed below are important telephone numbers and e-mail addresses:

	Telephone Numbers	*E-Mail Addresses*
Athletic office		
Attendance office		
Counselor's office		
Principal's office		

Listed below are important events and dates:

Events	*Date*
Open House	
Parent Conference Days	
First Quarter Report Card	
First Football Game	
First Cross-Country Meet	
First Volleyball Contest	

Sincerely,

Principal

Enclosures: Student Activity Calendar
            Student Handbook
            Reduced-Fee and No-Fee School Lunch Guidelines

Welcome Letter 6.5

PARENT(S) (3)

Secondary

(Date)

(Name)

(Address)

Dear (Name):

Welcome to (Name of School) School!

We are excited about the first day of school, (Date).

We would like all students and families to come to (Name of School), pick up their class schedules, find their classrooms, and meet their teachers at Open House on (Date).

Hot lunches will be served on the first day of school. The cost is (Dollar Amount) per meal. Money can be deposited into lunch accounts during Open House and every school day between (Time) and (Time) A.M. in the school cafeteria. All checks should be made payable to (Name of School). Students may also pay for their meals as they go through the line. Free and reduced-priced meals will be available to families who qualify. An application for free or reduced-price meals is enclosed in this packet. If your family qualifies for either free or reduced-priced meals, please complete the form and return it to the office *before* the first day of school or at Open House. *The school office cannot loan money.*

Please call if your (Son/Daughter) will be absent or tardy. Parents should call (Phone Number) between (Time) and (Time) A.M.

We look forward to a great year, and we hope to see you at Open House!

Sincerely,

Principal

Welcome Letter 6.6

PARENT(S) (4)

Elementary

(Date)

(Name)

(Address)

Dear (Name):

The (Name of School) School staff welcomes your child to the (Year) school year. The first day of school starts at (Time) on (Day of Week), (Date), and ends at (Time).

On the first day of school, your child should report directly to (His/Her) homeroom (Room Number). For the (Year) school year, a hot lunch will cost (Dollar Amount), or your child may bring a sack lunch.

We look forward to seeing your child(ren) on (Day of the Week), (Date).

Enclosed are the Emergency Information Card and the Student Handbook. Please return the emergency card and the student handbook receipt to the school on (Date). Also enclosed is a school calendar.

If you have any concerns about any aspect of your child's schooling, feel free to contact the teacher, a guidance counselor, or me. We welcome your inquiries.

We hope these materials are helpful to you. We look forward to a great school year!

Sincerely,

Principal

Enclosures: Emergency Information Card
              Student Handbook
              Calendar

Welcome Letter 6.7

PARENT(S) (5)

Kindergarten

(Date)

(Name)

(Address)

Dear (Name):

I hope you have enjoyed many summer activities! I hope, too, that your child is excited about coming to school on (Date).

Please have your child wear the enclosed name tag the first day of school. This is especially important if your child rides the bus.

Our regular time schedule is

AM Kindergarten	PM Kindergarten
8:45 to 11:30 A.M.	12:00 to 2:45 P.M.

The kindergarten teachers for the (Year) school year are (Name), (Room Number), and (Name), (Room Number).

We look forward to seeing you at Open House on (Date).

Sincerely,

Principal

Welcome Letter 6.8

PARENT(S) (6)

Kindergarten

(Date)

(Name)

(Address)

Dear (Name):

Welcome to (Name of School) kindergarten! We are looking forward to a great year with your child!

Following are the procedures for kindergarten students entering and leaving the school.

Where do kindergarten students enter the building? All kindergarten students enter the building from the (Direction). The teacher will meet the children at the door the first few weeks of school.

Where do kindergarten students wait to be picked up? Kindergarten students are dismissed at (Time) and (Time) from the (Direction) door. The teacher accompanies them to the main sidewalk and *NEVER* leaves them unattended until all children are picked up.

Please call (Phone Number) if you have any questions. We look forward to the start of school!

Sincerely,

Principal

Welcome Letter 6.9

PARENT(S) (7)

Elementary or Secondary

(Date)

(Name)

(Address)

Dear Parents:

This year, as some of you know, we have had a few changes in personnel. Two teachers are new to the faculty.

(Identify the new teachers and provide brief biographies.)

We are happy to welcome these new members. All are well qualified in their teaching disciplines, and I am sure they will enhance our fine faculty.

Sincerely,

Principal

Welcome Letter 6.10

NEIGHBORS

Elementary or Secondary

(Date)

(Name)

(Address)

Dear (Name):

The academic year for our students will start on (Day of the Week), (Date). The school day begins at (Time) A.M. and ends at (Time) P.M. With school buses and cars dropping off and picking up students, these are peak traffic times around (Name of School) School.

As in the past, we will attempt to keep the neighborhood clean. As you know, tips from neighbors can help us to deter suspicious activities. If you suspect problems, please call our office at (Phone Number) during the school day or call the Police Department at (Phone Number) after school hours.

Open House will be held on (Date). We hope you will stop by!

Sincerely,

Principal

Welcome Letter 6.11

STAFF (1)

Elementary or Secondary

(Date)

(Name)

(Address)

Dear (Name):

Welcome back to school. I hope you have had a great summer vacation. Our job at (Name of School) School is to help educate students. That task requires a real team effort. To begin building our team, we will have our first staff meeting of the school year on (Date) from (Time) to approximately (Time), in the school auditorium.

Lunch will be served in the cafeteria at 11:30 A.M.

During the afternoon, you can use your time to prepare for the opening of school.

Our program is what it is because of the dedicated educators such as you who work at our school.

I look forward to working with you and seeing you soon.

Sincerely,

Principal

Welcome Letter 6.12

STAFF (2)

Elementary

(Date)

(Name)

(Address)

Dear (Name):

Summer vacations provide time for rest and relaxation. I hope you are rejuvenated and ready for the start of a new year at (Name of School).

As the beginning of the new school year approaches, I look forward to opening day. Opening day offers excitement and promise for educators and students alike. When our students return to school on (Date), we will have a great opportunity to make a difference in their lives. Our array of talents, as faculty, have far-reaching effects toward establishing a rich and stimulating learning environment for the students of (Name of School).

Joining the (Name of School) team this year are (Name), Grades (Number); (Name), Grades (Number); and (Name), Grades (Number). I want to extend a welcome to our newly hired faculty on behalf of the staff and students of (Name of School).

To all of you: *Welcome Back!* I look forward to the (Year) school year and envision a year filled with excitement and many reasons to celebrate.

Please note the following meeting times:

(Day of Week), (Date), (Time), (Name of Meeting).

(Day of Week), (Date), (Time), (Name of Meeting).

See you then!

Sincerely,

Principal

Welcome Letter 6.13

STAFF (3)

Elementary

(Date)

(Name)

(Address)

Dear Staff:

I am looking forward to the new school year and hope you are too. Our first official day back is (Date).

Our first staff meeting of the year will be held on (Date). We will have a continental breakfast available at (Time). The meeting will start at (Time). I'm enclosing a calendar and handbook with this letter for your information.

I look forward to seeing you soon!

Sincerely,

Principal

Enclosures:

Welcome Letter 6.14

STAFF (4)

Elementary or Secondary

(Date)

(Name)

(Address)

Dear (Name):

Welcome to (Name of School) School. The staff, parents, and students feel that our school is the best in the state. We've received national recognition for student performance as well as for the outstanding teaching by our faculty.

We look forward to working with you at the teacher orientation program on (Date) at (Name of School) School. The agenda for the orientation program is as follows:

8:00 to 8:30 A.M.	Continental breakfast
8:30 to 8:45 A.M.	Welcome by the principal and staff
8:45 to 12:00 P.M.	New teacher orientation
12:00 to 1:00 P.M.	Lunch in school cafeteria
1:00 to 3:00 P.M.	Class preparation
3:00 to 3:30 P.M.	Meeting with principal, mentors

At the orientation, you will receive a staff handbook, curriculum guides, teacher textbooks, your room keys, and other materials.

Lunch will be served at 12 noon. At that time, your mentor teacher (Name) will join us. You and your mentor teacher will be able to work together during the afternoon preparing your classroom. Afterward, we will meet at 3:00 P.M. to discuss any questions you may have.

I look forward to seeing you soon.

Sincerely,

Principal

Welcome Letter 6.15

STAFF INFORMATION SHEET

Elementary or Secondary

(Date)

(Name)

(Address)

Dear (Name):

Staff Update: We welcome our new teacher, (Name).

Positions yet to be filled: (Positions)

Postcards: As most of you are aware, each year teachers send postcards to students in their homerooms to welcome them to the upcoming school year. This activity is a tradition at (Name of School). Labels for the postcards may be picked up in the office after (Date), or you may hand-address them. Teachers, please write out an extra card or two in case you have a new student. Please include your room number on the postcards. They are due (Date). Thank you!

First day back for teachers: (Date)

Open House will be: (Date)

Sincerely,

Principal

Welcome Letter 6.16

STAFF (5)

Elementary

(Date)

(Name)

Dear Staff:

I have the highest regard for the dedication, diverse talents, and skills of our staff and the effects they have on our students. I am impressed daily with your caring ways for students and staff.

I look forward to the (Year) school year and the exciting opportunities it will bring.

Sincerely,

Principal

Welcome Letter 6.17

TEACHER(S), FIRST YEAR

Elementary or Secondary

(Date)

(Name)

Dear (Teacher Name):

Welcome to (School). We hope you'll have an excellent first year at (School). To assist you with your transition to the new teaching position, (Name) has agreed to serve as your mentor. (Name) will be available to answer questions you may have and to assist you throughout the year.

In addition to your mentor, you will find that (Names), assistant principals; (Names), guidance counselors; and (Name), department chair will be great resources for you throughout the year.

The new faculty meeting is scheduled for (Date) in (Location) from (Time) to (Time). An agenda for the meeting will be sent to you soon.

Other new faculty meetings will be held on the following dates: (Dates). Please include these dates in your calendar since they are mandatory meetings.

If I can answer any questions you might have, please let me know. I am happy you have joined the faculty at (School). I look forward to observing your teaching accomplishments with our students!

Sincerely,

Principal

7

Information and Procedures Letters, Memos, Forms, and Announcements

Information and procedures letters provide direction and give guidance. Their ultimate aim is to provide clarity, eliminate confusion, and answer potential questions. Letters sent by the principal should be timely so that they are of maximum assistance to the school community. Information and procedures letters might be sent for the following reasons:

Staff safety concerns may require the sharing of information and procedural directions. Bus safety, fire safety, stranger danger, emergencies, and field trips are instances when letters to parents may be required.

Grading, achievement tests, and *athletics* may necessitate letters to parents or guardians.

Ordering supplies, gathering items for daily newsletters, preparing teaching portfolios, announcing upcoming changes, or *preparing news releases* are some of the reasons staff members might receive information or procedures letters.

Summer school, graduation, and the *end of the school year* are other events that require information and procedural letters for students, parents, and staff.

Information 7.1

PARENT(S), SAFETY (1)

Elementary

(Date)

(Name)

(Address)

Dear Parents and Guardians:

As you may have seen on television or heard on the radio, the police are seeking information about the driver of a van who approached children on their way to school this morning. The children responded appropriately and are safe. This is the third such incident that has occurred in our community in recent weeks. The police are investigating these incidents and will be monitoring the streets around the school.

This may be a good time to discuss safety issues with your children, particularly if they walk to and from school. Please review safety procedures with your children.

Sincerely,

Principal

Information 7.2

PARENT(S), SAFETY (2)

Elementary or Secondary

(Date)

(Name)

(Address)

Dear (Name):

As you may have already heard, school bus (Number), which your child rides, was involved in a minor accident at (Address) on (Date), at approximately (Time). I am pleased to report that no child was seriously injured.

If you want more information about this accident, please contact (School Office) at (Phone Number).

Sincerely,

Principal

Information 7.3

PARENT(S), SAFETY (3)

Elementary or Secondary

(Date)

(Name)

(Address)

Dear (Name):

As you may have heard, the fire department arrived at our school at approximately (Time) today. A fire was caused by (Means) in the (Place). All students and staff were safely evacuated.

Students and staff were out of the building for approximately 30 minutes. No major damage occurred to the school, and no one was injured. If you have any questions about the situation, please call me at (Telephone Number).

Sincerely,

Principal

Information 7.4

PARENT(S), BUILDING SECURITY

Elementary or Secondary

(Date)

(Name)

(Address)

To Parents and Guardians:

For the safety of all of our students, the doors to the school will remain locked during the school day. If you come to school during the day, please go to the (Location) entrance and use the intercom to communicate with the office staff. They will assist you in entering the building.

Everyone will be required to enter via the (Location) entrance. This includes parents, community members, visitors, volunteers, and district employees. Everyone must report to the office, sign in, and receive a visitor's badge. Everyone must sign out in the office as well.

Although this process may take more time and effort, it is designed to address concerns for the safety of our students. This procedure is uniform throughout the school district.

The district has installed security cameras at the entrances and in the hallways to address safety concerns.

In the interest of safety for all of our students, please observe these procedures when you visit the school.

Thanks for your assistance!

Sincerely,

Principal

Information 7.5

PARENT(S), INTERNET

Elementary or Secondary

(Date)

(Name)

(Address)

Dear Parents and Guardians:

Recent news reports highlight the dangers associated with unrestricted or unsupervised Internet use. Victims of cyber crime are not limited to young children. The news accounts suggest that adults, as well as youth, have been victims.

For our collective safety, please review your rules for Internet safety in your home. We will review the rules for Internet safety at school. These are the same rules you received and signed with your children at the beginning of the school year. If you would like to review those rules again, they are on the school Web site at (Web Address) or call (Name) at (Telephone Number) for a copy.

Although the Internet is an excellent resource, we must all be vigilant for those who prey on others through e-mail access and chat rooms. The students' safety is our number one concern.

Thanks for your attention to this issue!

Sincerely,

Principal

Information 7.6

PARENT(S), CONTAGIOUS ILLNESS

Elementary or Secondary

(Date)

(Name)

(Address)

Dear Parents and Guardians:

We have had (Number) cases of (Illness) reported by the parents of our students. As you know, (Illness) is highly contagious. It is spread by (Method). The common symptoms of this illness are (Symptoms).

If your child displays these symptoms, please talk to the child's doctor immediately. Please tell the doctor that (Illness) has been identified at the school.

We are required to keep the (State) Health Department informed of the illnesses reported to the school. The health department has been alerted to the (Illness) at (Name) School.

Please follow the guidelines provided by your doctor concerning when it is safe for your child to return to school if (He/She) is diagnosed with (Name) illness.

Sincerely,

Principal

Information 7.7

PARENT(S), DRUGS

Secondary

(Date)

(Name)

(Address)

Dear Parents and Guardians:

According to information we have received from a study conducted by Columbia University (www.casacolumbia.org), more teens are reporting the availability of drugs in their schools. Those who have access to drugs are more likely to try them.

The findings of the survey conducted by Columbia University indicated that teens who "viewed drugs as morally wrong" were less likely to try them. Similarly, teens who felt their parents would be "extremely upset" if they tried drugs were less likely to try them.

Teens who "confided in their parents" were at lower risk of drug use than those who confided in "other adults."

Once again, the paramount role of parents in the lives of their children has been reaffirmed. Although the schools and the community invest consistent and considerable resources in drug prevention and safety programs, we know that the parents are the best prevention program.

Continue to keep those communication channels with your teens open!

Sincerely,

Principal

Information 7.8

PARENT(S), PARTIES

Secondary

(Date)

(Name)

(Address)

Dear Parents and Guardians:

As our students get older, they increasingly find themselves at parties at their friends' houses or hosting parties in your home. Based on the stories we hear at school, we offer the following guide to teen parties.

First of all, parents need to understand the law as it relates to teens and parties. Parents are legally responsible for what happens to minors in their homes!

In order to create safe parties, consider the following: Before any invitations are extended, decide who will be invited, determine the starting and ending times for the party, and plan the activities for the party. Establish the rules before anyone is invited. Rules should include *no* drugs, *no* alcohol, *no* smoking, lights on, and limit the party area to specific spaces. Adults must be present during the party. Invite other parents to attend the party. This makes supervision easier and more enjoyable! Check on the teens regularly to make sure that these guidelines are being followed.

Parental responsibility in sponsoring a party is significant. Serving alcohol to minors or allowing minors to consume alcohol on your property can result in criminal charges. Drugs are illegal for everyone to possess or use.

By establishing guidelines and enforcing them, you can sponsor a safe and enjoyable party.

If you have any questions or need further information, please contact (Name) at (Telephone Number) or (E-mail).

Sincerely,

Principal

Information 7.9

PARENT(S), SUICIDE

Secondary

(Date)

(Name)

(Address)

Dear Parents and Guardians:

We are increasingly concerned about the safety of our students. One issue we are particularly attentive to is the potential for student suicide. For this reason, we have compiled the following list of concerns that we should all be attentive to as we work with students.

- Suicide attempts
- Written threats
- High level of depression
- Use of drugs/alcohol
- Socially withdrawn/isolated
- Verbalized suicide attempt
- Evidence of a suicide plan
- Displays of hopelessness

If you observe any of these behaviors, please seek professional help for your son/daughter immediately. The safety of your child is our highest concern. If you would like to discuss these issues with any school personnel please call (Name—Phone Number) or e-mail (Name—E-mail Address).

Sincerely,

Principal

Information 7.10

PARENT(S), MORNING ROUTINES

Elementary

(Date)

(Name)

(Address)

Dear Parents and Guardians:

Some parents have expressed concerns about establishing morning routines for their children to make the day go better for the whole family. Based on these conversations, you might want to review your morning routine.

The parents I spoke with reminded me of the following guidelines for "getting up and getting on it."

1. **Consistency.** Having a routine that is the same each day allows everyone to stay on track and on time. Expectations are clear, confusion is limited, and less time is wasted in the morning.

2. **Wake-Up Time.** The time to wake up is based on how much time it takes to roll out of bed and get ready for school. Once the necessary amount of time has been identified, add a cushion of perhaps 15 minutes, establish the wake-up time, and stick to it. Determine whether the parent or the alarm clock will provide the wake-up message.

3. **The Night Before.** Gathering books, papers, supplies, and backpacks the night before streamlines the morning scramble. Placing these items in the same place every evening reduces confusion. Picking clothes and placing them in the same location each evening may make the morning more peaceful. There may be more time for the struggles of decision making in the evening. If lunches need to be packed, they can be planned or organized in the evening.

4. **Breakfast.** The morning eating routine needs to be determined. Some students eat breakfast at school, some eat breakfast at home. The reports are consistent that breakfast is important in school performance. Determine who will make breakfast. Set guidelines for what constitutes a nutritious breakfast.

5. **Good-Bye.** Start the day on a positive note. Tell the children that you love them as you say good-bye. You can set the tone for a successful day!

Thanks to all who have shared their winning tips for making the morning routine more enjoyable in their homes. We hope these tips will be helpful to you!

Sincerely,

Principal

Information 7.11

PARENT(S), BEDTIME

Elementary

(Date)

(Name)

(Address)

Dear Parents and Guardians:

One topic that we hear mentioned frequently by parents is bedtime. At school we see what happens when students do not get enough sleep. Students have a hard time keeping up when they are tired.

Children need a regular bedtime and a regular bedtime routine. The bedtime should be based on the child's need for sleep and sleeping patterns.

It is good to have a planned routine for getting ready for bed and getting into bed. This may include bathing, brushing teeth, drinking a glass of water, saying good night, reading, or listening to music. Soothing, quiet activities may make the transition to sleeping easier.

If your child has a difficult time falling asleep or has nightmares, your involvement in the "soothing" activities may need to be more extensive. Reading with your child may provide additional assurance to your child at bedtime. A favorite toy or a nightlight may be comforting too.

Bedtime is a special time to be with a child. A good night's sleep helps everyone have a better day!

We hope these ideas are helpful to you and your children.

Sincerely,

Principal

Information 7.12

PARENT(S), SCHOOL AVOIDANCE

Elementary

(Date)

(Name)

(Address)

Dear Parents and Guardians:

The beginning of the school year may cause your child to exhibit anxiety about school attendance. School avoidance or school phobia may be prevalent. In fact, this behavior may be the manifestation of a fear of being separated from a parent. Your child may cry or resist going to school.

If this is the case, you might consider the following strategies:

- First of all, make it clear to your child that he or she must attend school.
- Spend time with your child, becoming familiar with the school, classrooms, lunchroom, and play areas.
- Consider walking to school in a group with other neighborhood children and parents (or carpool).
- Discuss the child's fears with teachers and support staff so that the child is supported and engaged in school activities.
- Involve the child in extracurricular activities so that the child's self-confidence is further developed.
- Arrange for someone other than the "attached" parent to take the child to school.

Remember, anxiety is a communicable emotion. If you display calm confidence, the child will receive that message. If a child's anxiety does not diminish, it may be time to seek professional counseling services.

Peers, patience, and consistency help! If I can help ease your child's anxiety, please contact me at (Telephone Number), (E-mail Address).

Sincerely,

Principal

Information 7.13

PARENT(S), HELPING KIDS

Elementary

(Date)

(Name)

(Address)

Dear Parents and Guardians:

Frequently we are asked by parents, "What can we do to help our kids?" Here are a few ideas we have gathered for you.

Help develop your children's social skills.

Take time to set good examples and teach children social skills and behaviors. Getting along with others is an essential social skill.

Take time to talk to your children.

Be a role model, talk about your feelings. Encourage discussion and conversation about feelings. This may defuse anger, sadness, and fear. You may reduce the number of tantrums or mood swings displayed by your children!

Celebrate accomplishments!

Reward your children for their accomplishments and good behavior. Emphasize the positives!

Curb the extracurricular activities.

Avoid creating stress for children by overinvolvement in activities. Children need personal time just as adults do!

We hope these ideas are useful to you!

Sincerely,

Principal

Information 7.14

PARENT(S), TRUTHFULNESS

Elementary

(Date)

(Name)

(Address)

Dear Parents and Guardians:

We appear to be experiencing a wave of lying at school. Perhaps you have noticed your child lying at home?

We know that there are a variety of reasons why children lie. These reasons include the following:

- To avoid punishment
- To avoid blame
- To protect themselves
- To get something they want
- To impress their peers
- To express their anger
- To be like their peers

We have been having conversations about truthfulness and trust at school. We have also discussed the importance of positive role models who tell the truth.

We hope that you will take time to teach about honesty in your family. Your example and interest in your child are the greatest influence in their lives. The children love to hear stories about you and your family, and the lessons you share through these stories will be lasting.

If a child has a severe problem with lying, it may be time to seek professional help. There may be an underlying issue that the child needs to address.

Thank you for your attention to this issue.

Sincerely,

Principal

Information 7.15

PARENT(S), SOCIAL WORKERS

Elementary or Secondary

(Date)

(Name)

(Address)

Dear Parents and Guardians:

You may know that our school district employs social workers. These individuals help meet the children's emotional, developmental, and educational needs.

The social workers provide a range of services to students, families, and school faculty in support of the children's needs. Services may include connection with community services, mental health services, crisis interventions, social skill development, and working with families, school staff, and students.

If you would like to contact a social worker and learn of the resources and services available to you, please call (Name) at (Telephone Number) or use e-mail (E-mail Address) to contact (Him/Her).

We are fortunate to have these services available to us!

Sincerely,

Principal

Information 7.16

PARENT(S), PARENT MENTOR PROGRAM

Elementary

(Date)

(Name)

(Address)

To Parents and Guardians:

We are implementing a Parent Mentor program this year. The purpose of the program will be to provide a parent contact for families who move to our school. As our society becomes more mobile, we have a steady stream of new students coming to our school. Providing a parent-to-parent connection for new families may ease the transition.

We hope you will become a Parent Mentor. The Parent Mentor's role is to greet the new family and welcome them to our school family; invite them to an upcoming school activity like Welcome Back Night or the Fall Festival; give the family your telephone number so they can call you if they have questions; call the family after the first week of school to see if they have any questions; and invite them to the Parent Association meetings.

We want new families to feel welcome and connected to the school. You can assist in this process by becoming a Parent Mentor. If you are willing to assist with this process, please let me know. You can reach me at (Telephone Number/E-mail Address).

Thanks for considering this opportunity!

Sincerely,

Principal

Information 7.17

PARENT(S), MIDDLE SCHOOL

Middle

(Date)

(Name)

(Address)

To Parents and Guardians:

We are pleased to have your child in (Name) Middle School this year. If you have not had a child in middle school or did not attend a middle school yourself, you may be interested in some of the terms we use to describe middle school practices. Among the terms you may hear are the following:

Team: A group of students who have the same teachers. The team might include language arts, math, science, special education, and social studies teachers.

Interdisciplinary Unit: A unit of instruction that involves more than one curricular area.

Flexible Block Schedule: Class periods are arranged and rearranged to support curricular objectives.

Student Assistance Team (SAT): A formal meeting to plan strategies to help a student. Meeting participants may include parents, guardians, student, teachers, counselor, and administrator.

Exploratory: Activities that extend learning through social, educational, and service learning experiences.

If you have any questions about middle school or your child's scheduling and learning activities, please contact me at (E-mail Address/Telephone Number). (Name) Middle School is a great place for students!

Sincerely,

Principal

Information 7.18

PARENT(S), FIELD TRIPS

Elementary

(Date)

(Name)

(Address)

Dear (Name):

Field trips are an important part of your child's education. Once again, we ask you to complete the enclosed form granting permission for your child to participate in a field trip.

The forms must be filled out, signed, and returned to the school prior to the trip. No student will be allowed on any trip without this signed and completed form. Teachers will not be allowed to make exceptions to this rule.

Thank you for your assistance.

Sincerely,

Principal

Information 7.19

PARENT(S), SCHOOL DEMOGRAPHICS

Elementary or Secondary

(Date)

(Name)

(Address)

To Parents and Guardians:

As we begin our new year at (School Name) School, we want you to have a "snapshot" of our school.

Our students include:

(Number) of students in grades (Grades)   (%) Special education students
Average class size (Number of Students)   (%) Mobility
(Number) of languages   (%) Eligible for free/reduced meals
(%) Students of color   (%) Average daily attendance
(%) English language learners

Our staff includes:

(Number) of teachers   (Number) Doctoral degrees
(Number) Master's degrees   (Number) Out-of-field teaching
(Number) Specialist certificates   (Years) Average years of teaching

Our school specialists include:

Art   Music
Computer   Physical Education
Counselor   Social Worker
Health   Special Education
Library   Speech-Language

We look forward to a great year for the students of (Name) School. If you have any questions, please contact me at (Telephone Number/E-mail).

Sincerely,

Principal

Information 7.20

PARENT(S), CONTACT INFORMATION

Elementary or Secondary

(Date)

(Name)

(Address)

Dear Parents and Guardians,

Welcome to (Name) School. We hope your children will have an excellent school year filled with opportunities, challenges, successes, and excitement.

Enclosed is the (Name) School handbook. Please review the handbook so that you are familiar with the (Name) School's policies and expectations.

If you have any questions concerning the policies and expectations, please contact a member of the administration or staff for answers to your questions.

School administrators you may want to meet include the following:

	Telephone Number	*E-Mail Address*
Principal: _____		
Associate Principal: _____		
Associate Principal: _____		
Associate Principal: _____		
Special Education Administrator: _____		

Best wishes for a great school year!

Sincerely,

Principal

Information 7.21

PARENT(S), WEATHER

Elementary or Secondary

(Date)

(Name)

(Address)

Dear Parents and Guardians,

As you know, the temperatures have set new record highs during the past two weeks. We are experiencing serious difficulties with our air conditioning. The age of the system is one of the contributing factors in the difficulties. School district officials are working on solutions to the situation.

Please listen to radio station (Radio Station) or television station (Television Station) or check the associated Web sites (Web Addresses) for early dismissals due to extreme heat.

Thank you for your assistance with any temporary disruptions of the school day.

Sincerely,

Principal

Information 7.22

PARENT(S), EMERGENCIES

Elementary

(Date)

(Name)

(Address)

Dear Parent or Guardian:

If severe weather or an emergency causes the early closing of school, we need to make sure that all students arrive at their destinations safely.

On the following form, please indicate what your child should do if school is dismissed early.

Thank you for your assistance in providing this information.

Sincerely,

Principal

Please detach and return to school by (Date).

Emergency instructions for

_____   _____

               (Student's Name)   (Room Number)

_____ Go directly home
_____ Go to day care provider
_____ Remain at school until picked up
_____ Take school bus (if your child is transported by bus each day)
_____ Other

_____   _____

    (Parent or Guardian Signature)   (Date)

Information 7.23

PARENT(S), SPRING FEVER

Elementary

(Date)

(Name)

(Address)

Dear Parents and Guardians,

At last, spring has arrived! As you know, it is much harder to keep the students' focus on academics when the beautiful weather is beckoning our attention. You, too, may be experiencing SPRING FEVER!

However, to whatever extent you can, please continue to encourage your children to be attentive to their school work. The last weeks of school require great effort from students since "the end is in sight!"

The great strides students have made this year can be lost in the final weeks of school if the students lose their focus.

As always, your help is appreciated!

Sincerely,

Principal

Information 7.24

PARENT(S), STUDENT PROGRESS

Elementary

Date

(Name)

(Address)

Dear Parents and Guardians,

We have had an excellent start to the new school year. Thank you for your efforts to prepare your children for the start of school.

Please continue to be attentive to your children's progress as the academic year evolves. Continue your dialogue with your children about the school day. Use questions such as "How was your day?" "Tell me all about it." "Do you have homework?" "What is your homework?" "What was the best part of your day?" "Who did you sit with for lunch?" If your children have recess try these questions: "Who did you play with?" "What did you play?" These are just ideas for starting the conversation each day. Soon your children will start the conversation themselves. If you can initiate the conversation as soon as you see your children each day, it will become part of a daily, "scheduled" event.

Make yourself known to your children's teachers. Your children will notice when you greet their teachers—and when their teachers know who you are!

Check on the academic progress of your children. Start early! Check the Web sites (Web Addresses) established by your children's teachers for this purpose. If you have questions or concerns, e-mail (E-mail Address) or call (Telephone Number) the teacher. If necessary, schedule a time to meet with the teacher.

We look forward to an excellent year with your children!

Sincerely,

Principal

Information 7.25

PARENT(S), GRADING PERIOD

Secondary

(Date)

(Name)

(Address)

Dear (Name):

The first grading period ends on (Date). We report student averages at this time to allow students and parents an opportunity to review progress.

If you are not satisfied with the progress indicated by this report, there are still three weeks before the end of the first grading period. Improvement is still possible.

Subject: _____ Current Average: _____

Comments: _____

Please sign this report and return it to the subject teacher. If you have questions or concerns about the progress described in this report, please call or e-mail (Name), the teacher, at (Phone Number) or (E-mail Address).

Sincerely,

Principal

_____

(Parent's Signature)

Information 7.26

PARENT(S), ACADEMIC PERFORMANCE

Elementary or Secondary

(Date)

(Name)

(Address)

Dear Parents and Guardians:

We are continuing our efforts to help improve (Student's Name)'s academic performance. I have asked members of the faculty and staff to collect and review information on (Student's Name)'s learning and behavior. The teachers, guidance counselor, school psychologist, school social worker, and other staff members may assist in observations, interviews, administration of behavior checklists, and other data collection.

Once the review is completed, we will schedule a meeting with you to discuss plans to meet (Student's Name)'s needs. Please contact me at (Telephone Number) (E-mail Address) if you have questions.

Sincerely,

Principal

Information 7.27

PARENT(S), EDUCATIONAL PHILOSOPHY

Elementary or Secondary

(Date)

(Name)

(Address)

Dear Parents and Guardians:

As a school community, we have spent considerable time developing and refining the educational philosophy for the school. We want to make sure that you have a copy of the philosophy statement which is attached to this letter.

Thank you for your involvement in the development of the philosophy statement. Your support of the educational process is essential to student success!

Sincerely,

Principal

Attachment:

Information 7.28

PARENT(S), TESTS AND STANDARDS—
NO CHILD LEFT BEHIND (NCLB)

Elementary or Secondary

Date

Name

Address

City, State Zip

Dear Parents and Guardians:

According to the (State) Department of Education, (Name) Public School has earned exemplary status for its academic accomplishments during the (Years) school year. This status reflects information submitted to the (State) Department of Education with regard to the (Name) State Standards and for the federal government's No Child Left Behind (NCLB) law, which measures Adequate Yearly Progress (AYP).

(Name) School had (Number/%) of its (Grade) students reach proficiency in math. The state average was (Number/%).

(Name) School had (Number/%) of its (Grade) students reach proficiency in writing. The state average was (Number/%).

These percentages exceed the percentages required by NCLB/AYP.

Adequate Yearly Progress was measured and reported in reading. (School) students met the requirements. In (Number) grade, (Number/%) of the students met the reading requirement.

To see the (Name) School report card, visit the Web site (Web Address). If you have any questions, please contact (Names) at (E-mail Addresses) or by telephone (Telephone Numbers).

Sincerely,

Principal

Information 7.29

PARENT(S), NO CHILD LEFT BEHIND (NCLB)

Elementary or Secondary

(Date)

(Name)

(Address)

Dear Parents and Guardians:

We would like to share the results of our progress in meeting the No Child Left Behind (NCLB) Annual Yearly Progress (AYP) objectives. We are evaluated annually on four objectives: test participation, graduation, and achievement levels in reading and mathematics. Districts that miss any of the four objectives for two or more years are labeled as districts identified for improvement. During the (Years) school year, (District) missed the annual progress objective(s) in (Objectives).

Our Adequate Yearly Progress Review Summary can be found at (Web Address).

If you would like more information about the NCLB annual objectives, please contact (Name) at (E-mail Address/Telephone Number).

Sincerely,

Principal

Information 7.30

PARENT(S), TEACHER QUALIFICATIONS

Elementary or Secondary

(Date)

(Name)

(Address)

Dear Parents and Guardians:

We are required by federal law to share with you the qualifications of the teachers in (Name) School. Questions you may ask include the following:

Is my child's teacher licensed to teach the grades or subjects assigned?

Has the state waived any requirements for my child's teacher?

What was the college major of my child's teacher?

What degrees does my child's teacher hold?

Are there instructional aides working with my child? If so, what are their qualifications?

All the teachers in (Name) School hold bachelor's degrees. (Number/Percentage) hold advanced degrees. All are licensed for their assignments. All of the instructional aides are qualified for their work.

If you would like additional information, please contact me at (E-mail Address/ Telephone Number).

Sincerely,

Principal

Information 7.31

PARENT(S), TESTS AND STANDARDS—WRITING ASSESSMENT

Elementary

(Date)

(Name)

(Address)

Dear Parents and Guardians:

Students in grades (Grades) will be participating in the statewide writing assessments on (Dates). Students will be writing narratives, descriptive essays, and persuasive narratives.

Throughout the school year, students have had practice writing experiences in each of the genres. During the assessment, students will write on two consecutive days. Each session will last (Minutes). On the first day, students are given the topic and asked to write a preliminary draft. Drafts will be revised and a final copy will be prepared on the second day.

Please encourage your children to do their best in the writing experience. A good night's sleep and breakfast are the best preparation for taking a test.

Thanks for your help!

Sincerely,

Principal

Information 7.32

PARENT(S), TESTS AND STANDARDS—ACHIEVEMENT TESTS

Elementary

(Date)

(Name)

(Address)

Dear Parents and Guardians:

On (Date), students in (Grades) will be participating in the (Name) Achievement Test. The purpose of this assessment is to determine your child's level of achievement in areas such as reading, writing, mathematics, science, and social studies. We will use the data from this assessment to determine which students would benefit from remedial instruction. This assessment will allow us to determine how achievement of students at (Name) School compares to other students their age nationally.

This assessment is required by state statute. All schools are required to participate in some form of standardized achievement testing. Results of your child's performance on the (Name) test will be sent home.

You can assist your children by encouraging adequate sleep the night before and a good breakfast prior to school. Please remind your children to give the test their best effort.

Thanks for your assistance in making this a positive experience for your children. If you have any questions, please contact me at (E-mail Address—Telephone Number).

Sincerely,

Principal

Information 7.33

PARENT(S), ACHIEVEMENT TESTS

Elementary

(Date)

(Name)

(Address)

Dear (Name):

Last (Month), the (Name of Test) Achievement Test was administered to your child at (Name of School) School.

This test is used as a tool to help measure the academic progress of your child and to discover strengths and weaknesses that could help us in meeting your child's educational needs.

Enclosed you will find a copy of your child's achievement test results. A summary report of the performance of all students in the district, as well as students throughout the United States, is also enclosed.

If you would like to discuss these results with (Name of Student's Teacher), please call (Phone Number). We hope this information is useful to you.

Sincerely,

Principal

Enclosure:

Information 7.34

PARENT(S), TESTS AND STANDARDS—NATIONAL ASSESSMENT OF EDUCATIONAL PROGRESS (NAEP)

Elementary

(Date)

(Name)

(Address)

Dear Parents and Guardians:

The students in Grade 4 will complete the (Year) National Assessment of Educational Progress (NAEP) on (Date). They will be assessed in either reading or math. NAEP is a congressionally mandated project overseen by the National Center for Educational Statistics to continuously monitor the knowledge, skills, and performance of the nation's children and youth. As the "Nation's Report Card," NAEP has measured and reported on a regular basis what America's fourth graders know and can do since 1969. The 90-minute test provides reliable student achievement profiles for educators and citizens.

We hope that all of our students will be able to participate.

Sincerely,

Principal

Information 7.35

PARENT(S), TESTS AND STANDARDS—STANDARDS

Elementary or Secondary

(Date)

(Name)

(Address)

Dear Parents and Guardians:

As you may already know, the (Name) District curriculum is guided by academic standards. These standards specify what students should know and be able to do at each grade level. Instruction is linked to the standards. Assessments are conducted to assure that the students are achieving the standards.

If you would like further information about the specific standards, instructional strategies, or assessments, please visit the Web site (Web Address) or call me at (Telephone Number).

Sincerely,

Principal

Information 7.36

PARENT(S), ATHLETICS (1)

Secondary

(Date)

(Name)

(Address)

Dear (Name):

Please sign the following form if you received and reviewed the athletic handbook and agree to the statement below. To be eligible to participate in interscholastic athletics, your child must return this form to the coach by (Date). The coach must also receive a completed physical form.

- -

We have received a copy of the (Name of School) School's Handbook for Athletics. We understand the stated policies, rules, and regulations and intend to abide by them.

I give permission for _____ to participate
(Student's name)

in _____.
(Sport)

_____   _____
Signature of Parent or Guardian   Date

_____   _____
Signature of Student   Date

Information 7.37

PARENT(S), ATHLETICS (2)

Elementary or Secondary

(Date)

(Name)

(Address)

Dear Parents and Guardians:

Athletics are vital aspects of school life. They are important to our student-athletes, our student body, the parents, the community, and our collective school pride.

We all know how important our support for the athletes and teams is to the success of the programs.

Keep in mind that coaches have to make many tough decisions in deciding who does and does not make a team. The coaches must determine the player's skill levels, the athlete's dedication to the program, and the athlete's willingness to play a specific role on a team. The coaches discuss these decisions with the individual athletes.

We have freshman, sophomore, and junior varsity teams that provide introductory training experiences for the athletes. These programs provide instruction and playing time for a significant number of students. These programs provide opportunities for the coaches to work with and observe the athletes as they refine their skills. Just as we support the athletes and the teams, we need to support the work the coaches accomplish with the students.

We have a fine reputation because of our collective efforts to be positive, supportive purveyors of good sportsmanship. Thanks for your efforts on behalf of the students.

Sincerely,

Principal

Information 7.38

PARENT(S), ATHLETICS (3)

Secondary

(Date)

(Name)

(Address)

Dear (Name):

This is to inform you that (Name of Student) is academically ineligible for all activities in accordance with (Page in Academic Handbook).

Academic Eligibility

The (Name of School) School has the following four requirements for participation in activities:

1. All participants must be in grades (Numbers), in regular attendance, and taking a minimum of (Number) credit hours in (Number) classes.

2. If a participant is taking (Number) credit hours, he or she must be passing (Number) credit hours to be eligible.

3. Eligibility will be determined each grading period.

4. If a student is not passing (Number) of (Number) classes during a grading period, then he or she will remain ineligible until the student's grades are high enough to be removed from the ineligible list.

If you have any questions, please call (Phone Number) or e-mail me at (E-mail Address).

Sincerely,

Principal

Information 7.39

STAFF, SUPPLIES

Elementary or Secondary

MEMORANDUM

TO: Staff

FROM: (Name), Principal

DATE: (Date)

RE: Ordering Supplies

You might want to order supplies early to avoid the end-of-semester rush.

Please note the following six points:

1. Supply orders are due (Date).
2. Use the requisition forms. Be sure to list the vendor on the form.
3. Please use the approved vendor catalogs.
4. The catalogs are in (School Office).
5. Figure in the cost of shipping and handling on orders from vendors. Make sure to check your figures.
6. The following items will be ordered by the office: printed forms, report cards, letterhead, and envelopes of all sizes.

If you have any questions regarding your orders, please check with (Name) or me.

Thanks.

Information 7.40

TEACHER(S), CALENDAR DEVELOPMENT

Elementary or Secondary

(Date)

(Name)

(Address)

Dear Parents and Guardians:

We are developing a tentative schoolwide calendar for the (Years) school year. This calendar will *NOT* be distributed to students. Please let me know the dates or proposed dates for school activities, events, and meetings. Indicate the students who will be invited to participate in these events, and the number of potential participants, and the number of potential spectators. Suggest the location for the activity and equipment needs that may be associated with the event.

This information will assist in the planning for these events. Our objective is to have well-planned activities, held in appropriate spaces, supported with proper equipment and resources. Your pre-planning is an essential component of calendar development and planning for the events.

Thanks!

Sincerely,

Principal

Information 7.41

FACULTY AND STAFF—TRAGEDY

Date

Dear Faculty and Staff:

As you may have heard on the radio or television, a tragedy involving (Number) of our students occurred at (Time) (Day). At this time, we do not know the full details of this fatal tragedy.

We will follow our established procedures for this type of crisis. The Grief Counseling Team will be available in the building throughout the week.

When further details of the families' plans are available, I will provide you with that information.

Sincerely,

Principal

Information 7.42

TEACHERS AND STAFF, DAILY NEWS

Elementary

DAILY NEWS

Date _____

Please post items of interest to the staff! We'll distribute the news before lunch.

_____

_____

_____

_____

_____

_____

_____

Staff Absences: _____

_____

_____

Dates to Remember: _____

_____

_____

Information 7.43

TEACHER(S), PARENT-TEACHER CONFERENCES

Elementary or Secondary

(Date)

To Teachers:

Parent-teacher conferences provide special opportunities to build positive working relationships with parents. As you approach the first conferences of the year, keep the following purposes in mind. Our goals are to

- Meet student needs
- Develop a working relationship with the parents and guardians
- Suggest how parents can help their children be successful in school
- Describe the school's goals, standards, and rules
- Explain the child's growth and progress in the academic areas
- Describe the child's social and emotional adjustment
- Recognize the importance of the parents' participation in the conference
- Encourage parents' involvement in the school community

The conferences provide an opportunity for us to showcase our great work with students. We should welcome the chance to be seen at our best!

Sincerely,

Principal

Information 7.44

TEACHER(S), SUPERVISION

Elementary or Secondary

(Date)

Dear Faculty,

As we begin the new school year, it is important for all of us to be attentive to the importance of supervision of students. Although there is an extensive section concerning this topic in the faculty handbook, I want to emphasize these reminders as we begin our work.

In your area of direct supervision, you are

1. Responsible for the safety and well-being of the students at all times
2. Responsible for maintaining visual and auditory connections with the students
3. Responsible for accounting for all students
4. Responsible for classroom management
5. Accountable for student behavior and seeking assistance as needed
6. Responsible for immediately reporting the presence of non-class members in the classroom

For more detailed guidance concerning supervisory expectations, please review the faculty handbook.

We need to be consistent as a faculty in our expectations for student behavior. Thanks for your efforts in enforcing our guidelines.

Sincerely,

Principal

Information 7.45

TEACHER(S), GOALS (1)

Elementary or Secondary

(Date)

Dear (Teacher's Name):

As you prepare for the (Dates) school year, each teacher is expected to establish goals in each of the following areas:

1. Planning and Preparation
   a. Knowledge of Curriculum and Pedagogy
      i. Content
      ii. State and District Curriculum Requirements
      iii. Methods of Instruction
   b. Knowledge of Students
      i. Characteristics of the Age Group
      ii. Approaches to Learning
      iii. Skills and Knowledge
      iv. Cultural Issues
   c. Assessment of Student Learning
      i. Standards
      ii. Instructional Goals
      iii. Uses in Planning Instruction
   d. Selection of Instructional Goals
      i. Needs of Diverse Population
      ii. Appropriate to Students Needs
   e. Design of Instruction
      i. Materials and Resources
      ii. Learning Activities
      iii. Grouping Practices
      iv. Lesson Structure

2. Learning Environment
   a. Culture for Learning
      i. Expectations for Learning
      ii. Positive Teacher-Student Interactions
      iii. Positive Student-Student Interactions
      iv. Expectations for Achievement
   b. Classroom Management
      i. Communication of Expectations for Learning and Behavior
      ii. Group Practices
      iii. Transitions
      iv. Student Behavior
      v. Time

Information 7.45 (Continued)

3. Instruction
    a. Principles of Learning
        i. Motivation
        ii. Participation
        iii. Knowledge of Learning
        iv. Retention of Learning
    b. Communication
        i. Clear Directions
        ii. Clear Procedures
        iii. Oral Skills
        iv. Written Skills
        v. Consistency
    c. Discussion
        i. Student Participation
        ii. Techniques to Engage Learners
        iii. Questioning Skills and Levels
    d. Student Engagement
        i. Structure and Organization
        ii. Planning Activities
        iii. Student Grouping
        iv. Use of Materials and Resources

4. Professional Role
    a. Engages in Growth and Development Activities
    b. Maintains Records
    c. Communication with Families
    d. Communication with Colleagues
    e. Collaboration
    f. Contributions to Profession
    g. Contributions to District
    h. Contributions to Community
    i. Contributions to Building

Please review these categories and identify the goals you will work on for the (Date) school year. Please send your goals to me by (Date). You and I are scheduled for our annual goal-setting discussion on (Date/Time) in Room (Number). I look forward to visiting with you soon.

Sincerely,

Principal

Information 7.46

TEACHER(S), GOALS (2)

Elementary or Secondary

(Date)

Dear Faculty:

As we approach the beginning of the school year, we once again have the opportunity to establish personal and professional goals for the academic year. Please take the time to prepare your goals for the year and submit them to me by (Date). Indicate how success in meeting your goals will be measured throughout the year.

Once I have received your goals, I will schedule a meeting with you to discuss your goals. I look forward to working with you this year in meeting these goals.

Sincerely,

Principal

Information 7.47

TEACHER(S), APPRAISAL

Elementary or Secondary

(Date)

To Teachers:

As part of the annual appraisal process, each teacher is required to identify five professional goals for the academic year. Please indicate, in the spaces below, your goals for the (Years) school year. Return this form to me by (Date).

If you have questions or want to discuss your goals with me, please let me know!

Sincerely,

Principal

GOAL 1: _____

GOAL 2: _____

GOAL 3: _____

GOAL 4: _____

GOAL 5: _____

Information 7.48

TEACHER(S), PORTFOLIO PREPARATION

Elementary or Secondary

MEMORANDUM

TO: (Name)

FROM: (Name), Principal

DATE: (Date)

RE: Portfolio Preparation

As you prepare your portfolios as part of the annual assessment process, please consider providing evidence of the following:

Professional associations you belong to and your specific activities within the associations

Indicators of teaching effectiveness (student evaluations, parent evaluations, examples of student work, student honors related to your instruction, self-assessments based on professional goals)

Student organizations you provide leadership for and the students' accomplishments

Professional development activities you have participated in this year, including courses, workshops, conferences, seminars, readings, visits to other sites, and so forth

Honors and awards you have received this year

Grant applications that have been submitted or funded

Special projects

Please submit your portfolio before our meeting on (Date).

Thanks for your help!

Information 7.49

TEACHER(S), PROFESSIONAL GROWTH

Elementary or Secondary

(Date)

(Name)

(Address)

Dear (Teacher):

Following are the results of my annual assessment of your continuous professional growth according to the standards established by our school.

1. Progress toward advanced degree work:
    Bachelor's +15 semester credit hours
    Master's
    Master's +30 semester credit hours
    PhD

2. Courses completed during (Year)

3. Workshops attended during (Year)

4. Attendance and contributions to department meetings

5. Attendance and contributions to faculty meetings

6. Evidence of continuous improvement of instruction

7. Evidence of continuous efforts to innovate

8. Evidence of responsiveness to student needs

9. Honors, awards, recognition

Congratulations on your accomplishments during the school year.

Sincerely,

Principal

Information 7.50

TEACHER(S), TIME MANAGEMENT

Elementary or Secondary

(Date)

To Teachers:

As we prepare to begin another school year, I want to recap some of the conversations we had about time management at the end of the last school year. In that discussion, we agreed that the following strategies may help us manage our hectic schedules.

1. Separate school and home.
2. Avoid taking schoolwork home by making the most of your time at school.
3. Eliminate time wasters during your preparation and break times.
4. Keep your calendar with you.
5. Update the calendar daily.
6. Schedule personal time in the calendar.
7. Check e-mails at the end of day.
8. Handle e-mail only once.

If you have other time management strategies we should discuss, please let me know.

Sincerely,

Principal

Information 7.51

TEACHER(S), SPECIAL THANK YOU

Elementary or Secondary

(Date)

Dear (Teacher's Name):

In the course of my work in our building today, I noted that you deserve A Special "Thank You"

For your continued support

For your positive attitude

For your cooperation

For your attention to reports

For your loyalty to (Name) School

For your consideration and dedication to students

For the improvement of (Name) program

For _____

Sincerely,

Principal

Information 7.52

TEACHER(S), SPECIAL RECOGNITION

Elementary or Secondary

(Date)

Dear (Teacher's Name):

As I was working in our building today, I observed that You Deserve Special Recognition

For your kindness to students

For your support of staff

For your dedication to quality

For your professionalism

For your creative instruction

For your special efforts

For attending extracurricular activities

For _____

Sincerely,

Principal

Information 7.53

TEACHER(S), YOU WERE MISSED

Elementary or Secondary

(Date)

Dear (Teacher's Name):

I just wanted you to know that You Were Missed

    At your assigned duty station

    At inservice

    At the faculty meeting

    At a parent conference

    During an assembly

    At _____

Sincerely,

Principal

Information 7.54

TEACHER(S), PROTECTION

Elementary or Secondary

(Date)

Dear (Teacher's Name):

During my morning walk-through of the building, I noted that (describe the concern). For your protection, please abide by the following procedures:

Never leave students unattended

Mark student attendance in each class

Stand by the doorway during class changes

Report to assigned duty on time

Keep accurate records

Turn in lesson plans on time

Organize assignments for teacher absence

_____

Sincerely,

Principal

Information 7.55

STAFF, STUDENT MOBILITY

Elementary or Secondary

(Date)

To Teachers and Support Staff:

As you have observed in the classrooms, we have a high student mobility rate in our building and in our school district as a whole. Based on data provided by the central office, we know the district mobility rate is (Number of Students/%) and our building's mobility rate is (Number of Students/%). You have been diligent in your efforts to meet the needs of all of the students in this transitory environment. The national demographics suggest that we will continue to be challenged by the mobility of families.

As a group, we should focus our thinking and strategies for helping students adjust to their changes in school environments. Based on the number of students who have transitioned to the school in the past five years, we should be able to compile an impressive array of techniques that have been effective with the students. Helping students adjust to new teachers, new students, new routines, new expectations, new books, new communities, new customs, and a new school culture are among the types of experiences we have had. Helping students feel successful is possibly our hallmark!

Please give some thought to your techniques that work with our students-in-transition. E-mail your techniques or strategies to me. I'll combine the information, sort it by category, and we'll use it as the basis for our meeting on (Date).

Thanks for your assistance with this topic.

Sincerely,

Principal

Information 7.56

TEACHER(S), HOMEWORK

Elementary or Secondary

TO: Teacher(s)

FROM: Principal

DATE: (Date)

RE: Homework for (Student Name)

The above-named student is absent from school today. The parents/guardians called requesting that the student's assignments be assembled for pick-up after school today.

Please place the assignments in the homework and assignments tray in Room (Number) by (Time) today.

Thank you for your attention to this student's needs!

Information 7.57

SUBSTITUTE TEACHER(S), EXPECTATIONS (1)

Elementary or Secondary

(Date)

(Name)

(Address)

To Substitute Teachers:

Following is a list of expectations for substitute teachers in (Name) School:

- Follow the prescribed lesson plans for each class.
- Provide supervision of the students during class, transition periods, and dismissal times. Student safety is an important responsibility for *all* teachers.
- At the end of the day, straighten the classroom and arrange the student work and lesson plans.
- Sign out at the office. The school day ends at (Time).
- Remember, the computer equipment is for student instruction only. Any other use is strictly prohibited.
- Model professional behavior at all times!

Please adhere to these expectations during your work in (Name) School.

Sincerely,

Principal

Information 7.58

SUBSTITUTE TEACHER(S), EXPECTATIONS (2)

Elementary or Secondary

(Date)

(Name)

(Address)

To Substitute Teachers:

We are pleased you will be joining us as a teacher at (NAME) School today. We hope our students will have a productive learning experience during the time that you are with them.

You may have already received a list of expectations for substitute teachers. If you have not, we want to remind you that the following are minimum expectations for teachers in (Name) School.

- Be on time to your assigned classes and classrooms.
- Supervise students during class, passing periods, and dismissal.
- Follow the lesson plans provided.
- Respond professionally to those in authority.
- Respond professionally to co-workers.
- Treat students respectfully and professionally.
- Dress appropriately according to the guidelines in the substitute teacher handbook.
- Follow district policies.
- Use district equipment and property carefully and for instructional purposes only.
- Follow safety procedures.

We hope you'll have an excellent teaching experience today!

Sincerely,

Principal

Information 7.59

SUBSTITUTE TEACHER(S), CONFIDENTIAL INFORMATION

Elementary or Secondary

(Date)

(Name)

(Address)

Dear (Name):

Just a reminder, all student information you have access to during the school day is confidential. This information may not be discussed with anyone other than the school administrators, (Names). The same confidentiality rule pertains to any test data you may have access to during your time in (Name) School.

Thank you for your attention to this reminder!

Sincerely,

Principal

Information 7.60

STAFF, BEHAVIOR SPECIALIST

Elementary or Secondary

(Date)

Dear Faculty and Staff:

The role of the Behavior Specialist is to work with students, parents, staff, and administrators to assess the social and emotional needs of students and to assist with the development of positive behavioral support plans. (Name(s)), Behavioral Specialist(s), are available to assist and consult with building level staff to aid in designing positive behavioral support plans for students. These individuals should be contacted once building level expertise and resources such as the Student Assistance Teams (SAT), educational consultant, school psychologist, and school counselor have been used.

Requests for assistance should be submitted following the formal referral process. All involved personnel should be encouraged to participate in the process including the principal, classroom teacher(s), special education teacher(s), educational consultant, and school psychologist. Parents and guardians need to be notified as part of this process.

Sincerely,

Principal

Information 7.61

PARENT(S), CALENDAR

Elementary or Secondary

(Date)

(Name)

(Address)

Greetings!

Attached is a calendar of events for (Month). As you know, the calendar is subject to change. For the most up-to-date schedule information, please check (Name) School's Web site at (Web Address). For athletics and activities updates, please check (Web Address) for game information, cancellations, postponements, and schedules. The link also provides maps to game and activity sites.

We hope to see you at the school activities!

Sincerely,

Principal

Information 7.62

PARENT(S), UPCOMING CHANGES

Elementary or Secondary

(Date)

(Name)

(Address)

Dear (Name):

I have scheduled a special meeting to provide information and answer questions you might have about the changes planned for the school in the future. My purpose is to provide you with as much information as I can. You deserve to hear information directly from me.

We will do everything we can to address the changes in a sensitive and supportive manner.

I look forward to meeting with you on (Day of Week), (Date), at (Time). I hope you will attend.

Sincerely,

Principal

Information 7.63

TEACHER(S), NEWS RELEASE

Elementary or Secondary

PREPARING A NEWS RELEASE FOR THE PRESS

Keep the following in mind as you craft any news release:

How will I "grab" the reporter's attention?

Did I answer the who, what, when, where, and how questions?

Does the information appear in order of importance?

Did I keep it brief and to the point?

Are the facts and spelling accurate?

Did I avoid jargon and technical terms?

Information 7.64

PARENT(S), PROM

Secondary

(Date)

(Name)

(Address)

Dear Parents and Guardians:

As you already may know, Prom is (Date). Post-Prom starts at midnight, right after the Prom, and ends at (Time). The Prom will be held at (Location) and the Post-Prom will be held at (Location).

For the Post-Prom, the (Location) will be decorated and arranged to provide an exciting, fun-filled atmosphere for the special activities that have been planned. Among the many activities will be games, an obstacle course, karaoke, card games, music, dancing, and food. Prizes are a major feature and attraction of Post-Prom!

As a parent or guardian, you can help by doing the following:

1. Remind your junior or senior to purchase a ticket to Post-Prom. Tickets cost (Dollars) and will be sold (Dates) during (Times) at (Location).
2. Make a donation! Please consider making a donation to cover the expenses of Post-Prom. Donate a prize that will be given to a student during the evening either at a game or through one of the drawings that are held throughout the evening.
3. Volunteer to help. There are many volunteer opportunities available to you. Consider selling tickets, soliciting prize donations, decorating, picking up donated prizes, working at Post-Prom, or taking down the decorations.

Post-Prom has been a great, fun-filled, memorable activity for our students. It has been an exciting, drug-free, alcohol-free, supervised activity that the students look forward to each year. Our collective efforts in planning the activities, funding the event, and providing "incentive to stay" prizes have been great successes. We look forward to another great event and appreciate the contributions you will make to its success!

The person to contact with your questions, donations, and offers to volunteer is (Name, Telephone Number, E-mail Address).

Sincerely,

Principal

Information 7.65

PARENT(S), SUMMER SCHOOL

Secondary

(Date)

(Name)

(Address)

Dear Parents and Guardians:

We are beginning the planning for the Summer School schedule. As you know, Summer School may be a good option for a number of reasons. If a student has done poorly in a class or failed a class, this is an opportunity to correct that situation. Summer School also provides flexibility for students who want to fit more courses into their schedules. Summer School provides the opportunity to catch up and keep up.

The Summer School sites for this summer are (School Names). The Summer School hours are (Times).

We are extremely pleased to be able to offer a full range of courses during the summer. The scheduling of Summer School classes is contingent on enrollments. To register for a Summer School class, please visit a school counselor, or go to the Summer School link at (Web Address). In order to assist in the scheduling and provision of classes, please register by (Date).

We recommend the Summer School program to anyone who

1. Has failed a graduation requirement

2. Has done poorly, or failed, in a class that serves as a foundation for an upper-level course

3. Needs to earn additional credits

4. Needs the scheduling flexibility that the summer program offers

Please check the school Web site (Web Address) for more information about Summer School!

Sincerely,

Principal

Information 7.66

PARENT(S) OR GUARDIAN(S), SUMMER SCHOOL

Elementary

(Date)

(Name)

(Address)

Dear (Name):

Previously, we had discussed the possibility of (Name of Student)'s repeating the (Number) grade. When a student does not make adequate progress, grade repeating becomes necessary.

The alternative is for (Name) to attend summer school in (Month) and (Month). Successful completion of summer school will result in promotion to (Number) grade.

Summer school meets (Days of the Week) from (Time) to (Time) at (Name of School) School. The fee for summer school is (Dollar Amount).

To register for summer school, please contact (Name) by telephone (Phone Number) or by e-mail (E-mail Address).

Sincerely,

Principal

Information 7.67

PARENT(S) OR GUARDIAN(S), GRADUATION

Secondary

(Date)

(Name)

(Address)

Dear (Name):

The high school class of (Year) is scheduled to graduate on (Day of the Week), (Date), at (Time) at (Place). The public is invited to attend the ceremony.

Each senior must arrive at (Place) by (Time). Graduates only will assemble in (Place) before the graduation ceremony.

The (Place) will be open for seating at (Time). Individuals with disabilities will have access to seating in (Area).

Caps and gowns will be worn for graduation. Caps and gowns can be picked up on (Day of Week), (Date), from (Time) to (Time) in the (School Office).

Graduation is a formal event. Proper behavior is expected of all in attendance. Do not bring noisemakers or other distracting items into the (Place).

A professional photographer will take a picture of each graduate as the diploma is presented. A video of the graduation ceremony is also being produced. The picture and video will be available for purchase from the professional photographer. Personal pictures may also be taken in the specially designated area near the stage. Please do not disrupt the ceremony when taking pictures.

Diplomas will be available immediately following the ceremony in (Room Number).

Students who have not completed all requirements for graduation will not receive a diploma.

If you have questions about graduation, please call (School Office) at (Phone Number) or send an e-mail (E-mail Address).

Sincerely,

Principal

Information 7.68

STUDENT(S), GRADUATION

Secondary

SENIORS' END-OF-THE-YEAR REMINDERS

Commencement Practice: Practice for commencement will be held on (Date) from (Time) to (Time) in (Location).

Lockers: Locks must be turned in at the office. If a lock is not returned, there is a (Dollar Amount) fine. Seniors will be expected to clean their lockers prior to the last day of school, (Date).

Last Day of School: The last attendance day for seniors is (Date). Make sure that your class work is finished, all fines are paid, and that your record is clear before this time.

Senior Responsibilities: Any senior who has not fulfilled *ALL* responsibilities will not be awarded a diploma at commencement. Responsibilities include academic work completed, books checked in, fines paid, and locks returned.

Commencement: The (Name of School) High School (Year) Commencement is scheduled at (Location) at (Time), (Day of the Week), (Date). Plan to arrive at the (Location) by (Time) that day. Caps and gowns must be worn.

Information 7.69

STUDENT(S), END OF YEAR (1)

Secondary

(Date)

(Student Name)

(Address)

Dear (Student Name):

Congratulations on the completion of the (Year) year at (Name of School).

School Calendar: The (Next Year) Year School Calendar is enclosed. The first day of student attendance will be (Day of the Week), (Date).

Changes in Address: If your permanent mailing address changes, please notify us immediately. You will want to receive the special summer mailings as well as your (Next Year) class schedule.

Reminder to Athletes: Physical examinations are valid for one school year only. You might want to schedule appointments for your physical exams now. No athletic equipment will be issued or participation of any type allowed until physical examination and parent consent forms are completed. These forms may be obtained in the (School Office) Office throughout the summer.

Summer Office Hours: The (School Office) Office will be open Monday through Friday from (Time) to (Time) throughout the summer. If you need information or help, please come in or call us at (Phone Number).

Best wishes for a pleasant summer.

Sincerely,

Principal

Information 7.70

STUDENT(S), END OF YEAR (2)

Secondary

CHECKOUT

Student End of Year

Name: _____

This form is to be completed and turned into the principal's office before you are cleared for promotion or graduation. This form is due by _____.

(Date)

Period	Class	Books Checked In	Book Fines Paid	Work Completed	Teacher Initials
1					
2					
3					
4					
5					
6					
7					
8					

Information 7.71

PARENT(S), END OF YEAR

Elementary

(Date)

(Name)

(Address)

Dear (Name):

I'm sure you'll want to join me in saying *Thank you, (Name).* A huge thank you goes to (Name) for donating (Item) for the (Name of School). Congratulations to (Name), (Name), (Name), and (Name), the winners of the (Prize).

Next Year's Plans: Please notify the office (Position) if your child will *not* be attending (Name of School) next year.

Field Day: Our field day is scheduled for (Day of the Week), (Date), (Time). Please contact the office if you would be able to volunteer for one or two hours to run a game or activity. The rain date is (Date).

Year Account: Our cafeteria staff will be working with students to use up the balance in their (Year) accounts. If your child's account is depleted, with only a few school days left, we suggest you send cash.

At the end of the school year, any (Type) accounts that contain less than $2.00 will be automatically cleared without a refund. Accounts with a balance over $2.00 will have refunds available on request in the school office through (Date), then in the Accounting Department at (Name of District) District Office until (Date). Any unclaimed balances in the accounts will revert back to the (Name of Account).

Information 7.71 (Continued)

Dates to remember:

Date:	School Event
	Concert
	PTO Meeting
	No School
	Field Day
	No School
	Field Day (Rain Date)
	Report Cards Sent Home
	Last Day of School

Change of Address: Please notify the office of any address changes so that you will receive summer mailings promptly.

Sincerely,

Principal

Information 7.72

TEACHER(S), END OF YEAR (1)

Elementary or Secondary

TO: Teaching Staff

FROM: (Name), Principal

DATE: (Date)

RE: Next year's calendar, last days of school, and staff checkout

Next Year's Calendar

If you have any special events planned for next year, please submit the proposed date before you leave for the summer. We will prepare a master calendar for next year so that when you are planning a special activity, you will know if it conflicts with any other activity.

Last Days of School

Let's make the last days of this school year as positive for students as this school year has been for them already. Please be aware of the guidelines for showing movies, and make sure any movie you show is part of your overall curriculum plan. I will be reminding students about nuisance items during the last days of school. Please help with these reminders and be on the lookout also for any inappropriate items. Turn them into the office if anything is found or taken from a student.

Hall Supervision

Please help with hallway supervision and be as visible as possible to the students during these last (Number) days of school.

Staff Checkout

Staff will need to be completely ready to check out on (Date). We will provide more information about checkout as soon as possible.

Information 7.73

TEACHER(S), END OF YEAR (2)

Secondary

FACULTY CHECKOUT

Tasks	Initials	
1. All grades recorded on the report cards	Checked by:	
2. Books, audio, and video materials returned to the library	Checked by Librarian:	
3. Grade books turned into the building principal	Checked by:	
4. Classrooms clean—Checked by building principal	Checked by:	
a. No pictures or posters on bulletin boards or walls	Checked by:	
b. Bookshelves clean and emptied	Checked by:	
c. Desk clean and everything put away	Checked by:	
5. Inventories turned in to the building principal	Checked by:	
6. All keys returned and verified against key list	Checked by:	
7. Room repairs list turned in to _____.	Checked by:	
8. Athletic inventory turned in to athletic director	Checked by:	
9. Athletic budget turned in to athletic director	Checked by:	
10. Summer address:	Name:	Telephone #:
Checkout time:		

Information 7.74

TEACHER(S), END OF YEAR (3)

Secondary

Teacher's Sign-Out Sheet

Name: _____

1. Grade book in the principal's office   _____

2. Room cleaned   _____

3. Inventory turned in to the principal's office   _____

4. Keys and key identification list returned to   _____

5. Repair list turned in to   _____

6. Coaches: All equipment and inventory turned in to athletic director   _____

Information 7.75

PARENT(S), TALENT SHOW

Elementary or Secondary

(Date)

(Name)

(Address)

Dear Parents and Guardians:

Each year the students have enjoyed the opportunity to showcase their various talents in the annual variety show. Students who are interested in trying out for the show this year should note the following details about the tryouts.

- Sign-Up—Turn in the attached sign-up form no later than (Date) to the box marked "Tryouts" in the school office.
- Tryouts—Will be held after school in the Activity Center. Each student or group of students will be given a tryout time and date. Tryout dates are (Dates).
- Student Notifications—Decisions about who will perform in the show will be announced on (Date).
- Variety Show—The show will be held on (Date) in the (Location) at (Time).
- Performance Categories—Performance categories include instrumental music, vocal music, dance, skits, comedy, or speeches (No lip-synching).
- Guidelines:
  - All acts must be ready by the tryout.
  - Costumes and props must be used for tryouts.
  - Tapes must be queued to the exact start of the performance.
  - Acts and costumes must be appropriate and in good taste.
- No changes—No changes may be made in a performance after tryouts without the permission of the Show Director (Name).
- Parents—Parents are asked *not* to attend tryouts. Parents are encouraged to attend the show on (Date).

Thank you for supporting the students in this exciting showcase of their talents!

Sincerely,

Principal

Information 7.75 (Continued)

Variety Show Sign-Up Form

Student Name: _____   Grade/Room: _____

Other Students in Act: _____

Type of Performance: _____

Description of Performance (include title of music and artist): _____

_____

_____

_____

_____

_____

I have read the detailed information in the letter sent with this form and give my child permission to try out for the Variety Show.

Student Signature: _____

Parent Signature: _____

Date: _____

8

Discipline Letters and Forms

Discipline is an important aspect of a principal's role. Letters and documentation of discipline concerns are often prescribed by school district policies and contained in school district policy manuals. In serious instances, state statutes may determine a principal's response to a discipline problem. A school district attorney also may be involved in responding to discipline concerns.

Documentation of discipline problems is an important administrative responsibility. Addressing school discipline concerns requires an accurate accounting of the sources and types of discipline infractions. Letters and documentation of discipline problems might include the following:

Discipline referrals are reported to parents and documented in the principal's office.

Student discipline interventions may be documented in a discipline log.

Tardies, discipline infractions, and *behavior warnings* are reported to parents and copies of the letters maintained in the appropriate files.

Bus misbehaviors may require letters to parents, and copies of these letters should be placed in an appropriate file.

Student suspensions are accompanied by letters to parents. Copies of suspension letters should be placed in appropriate school files.

Discipline Form 8.1

REFERRAL

Elementary or Secondary

STUDENT DISCIPLINE REFERRAL

Name: _____   Grade: _____

Date: _____   Teacher: _____

Referral Initiated by: _____

Discipline Problem—check behavior(s) applicable:

A. Student-student	
B. Student-staff	
C. Violation of school rules	
D. Repeated violations of rules or referrals	
E. Attendance	
F. Bus behavior	
G. Other	

Parent Contact (choose one):

Phone _____   Conference _____   Letter _____

Action: _____

_____

Removal From School (choose one if applicable):

Rest of day _____   One or more days _____   Expulsion _____

Comments: _____

_____

Discipline Form 8.2

STUDENT BEHAVIOR RECORD

Elementary or Secondary

OFFICE INTERVENTION LOG

Name: _____

Date	Class	Behavior	Consequence(s)	Parent Contact[a]

a. Parent contact: 1 = phone; 2 = letter, report; 3 = conference

Discipline Letter 8.3

PARENT(S), TARDIES

Elementary or Secondary

(Date)

(Name)

(Address)

Dear (Name):

(Name of Student) has been tardy to class (Number) times since the beginning of the school year. Although we realize that emergencies occur on occasion, we expect students to arrive at school on time. It is important for (Name) to receive all the instruction that is available to (Him/Her). Also, it is disruptive for the class and instruction when a student arrives late. It is often difficult for a child to enter a room when (He/She) is late. Currently, the state statute regarding tardiness states the following: (Statute).

We would appreciate your assistance in helping (Name) arrive at school on time.

Sincerely,

Principal

Discipline Letter 8.4

PARENT(S), INFRACTION

Elementary or Secondary

(Date)

(Name)

(Address)

Dear (Name):

Your child has a discipline infraction of (Description of Infraction). This is the (Number) offense. As per the (Name of School) manual, the consequences will be (Description of Consequences).

If you have any questions about this situation, please refer to page (Number) of the (Name of School) manual.

Sincerely,

Principal

Discipline Letter 8.5

PARENT(S), WARNING

Elementary or Secondary

(Date)

(Name)

(Address)

Dear (Name):

During the past few days, several students have acted or made comments that have been inappropriate. Your (Son/Daughter), (Name), has acted in this manner.

The involved students have been told that if similar situations recur, detentions or suspensions from school may be the consequences. The inappropriate behavior and comments may be perceived as sexual harassment and are not tolerated by our school district. Page (Number) of the Student Handbook provides specific information about district policies.

We would appreciate your assistance in talking with (Name) about this behavior and the potential consequences if the behavior persists.

If you have any questions, please contact me.

Sincerely,

Principal

Discipline Letter 8.6

PARENT(S), BUS BEHAVIOR (1)

Elementary or Secondary

(Date)

(Name)

(Address)

Dear Parents and Guardians:

This is a reminder about student behavior on the bus. Any student behavior that causes the bus driver to divert (His/Her) attention from driving the bus is a serious violation of bus rules. These behaviors include the following:

1. Not obeying driver or safety rules
2. Distracting driver (yelling, being loud)
3. Disrespect (rude, discourteous)
4. Vandalism, theft
5. Out of assigned seat
6. Eating/drinking
7. Throwing objects
8. Weapon possession
9. Verbal abuse, threats, profane language
10. Possession of drugs, alcohol, or tobacco
11. Assault/battery, fighting, hazing, hitting

Please remind your child(ren) of the behavior expectations.

Consequences of misbehavior may include the following:

1. Verbal warning by bus driver
2. Referral to the principal; parents/guardians notified
3. Loss of bus privileges for a week
4. Loss of bus privileges for remainder of semester
5. Immediate removal, when the student's behavior is a threat to the other passengers

As you know, our goal is the safety of all of our students. Your help is essential if we are to achieve this goal.

Sincerely,

Principal

Discipline Letter 8.7

PARENT(S), BUS MISBEHAVIOR (2)

Elementary

(Date)

(Name)

(Address)

Dear (Name):

Today on the bus, (Name of Student) (Describe Behavior). I reviewed the situation with (Him/Her). (Name of Student) agreed that (He/She) broke a bus rule and was aware of the consequences of (His/Her) actions.

According to district procedures, students who are reported to the principal for misbehavior on the bus will receive a verbal warning, and a letter will be sent to the parents following the first offense. If a second offense occurs, however, a two-day suspension of bus privileges may be imposed following parent contact.

Please discuss this incident with (Name of Student), and thank you for your support of our efforts to provide safe transportation for students. If you have questions, please feel free to call me at (Phone Number).

Sincerely,

Principal

cc: Transportation Director
        Bus Driver
        Teacher
        Guidance Counselor
        File

Discipline Letter 8.8

PARENT(S), BUS MISBEHAVIOR (3)

Elementary

(Date)

(Name)

(Address)

Dear (Name):

Your (Son/Daughter), (Name of Student) has been reported for misbehavior on the school bus (Number) times this year. According to the Student Handbook, (Page Number), such referrals result in suspension from riding the school bus. Thus (Name of Student) is suspended from riding the school bus as of (Day of the Week), (Date).

In accordance with (Name of District) School District procedures, it will be necessary for you to meet with (Name of Student), the bus driver, and me before bus-riding privileges can be restored. Please contact me at (Phone Number) to arrange a convenient meeting time.

Sincerely,

Principal

Discipline Letter 8.9

PARENT(S), BUS MISBEHAVIOR (4)

Elementary

(Date)

(Name)

(Address)

Dear (Name):

We regret to inform you that (Name of Student)'s bus-riding privileges have been suspended from (Date) to (Date). When a situation arises that endangers the safety of other students, it is necessary for the school to take appropriate measures to correct it.

The reason or reasons for this suspension of bus privileges are as follows: (Description of Infraction).

If you have any questions, please feel free to call me at (Phone Number).

During the suspension, it is the responsibility of the parents to provide transportation.

Sincerely,

Principal

Discipline Letter 8.10

PARENT(S), SUSPENSION (1)

Elementary or Secondary

(Date)

(Name)

(Address)

Dear Parents and Guardians:

This letter is to inform you that your child (Name), has been suspended, out-of-school (OOS), for (Number) days. The suspension begins on (Date). (Name) may return to school on (Date). Students assigned to OOS are not allowed to come on school property or to attend any extracurricular activities on the days of suspension.

Please note the referral date (Date) for (Offense). This infraction is cited on page (Number) in the (Name) Student Handbook. Students on short-term suspension may make up work assigned on the days of suspension for partial credit. A maximum of (Percentage) will be allowed for each assignment successfully completed.

Your support in this matter is appreciated. Thank you for finding the time to speak with me on the telephone this afternoon. If you have any questions or concerns, please call me at (Number) or e-mail me at (E-mail Address).

Sincerely,

Principal

Discipline Letter 8.11

PARENT(S), SUSPENSION (2)

Elementary or Secondary

(Date)

(Name)

(Address)

Dear (Name):

(Name of Student) has been suspended from classes at (Name of School) School for a period of (Number) days. The suspension will be an in-school suspension and will be served (How Served) through (Date). (Name of Student) is to report to the In-School Suspension Room (Room Number) at (Time) and will be released at (Time).

While on suspension, (Name of Student) will be expected to complete assignments from (His/Her) teachers each day. The class work completed will be returned to the teachers and full credit given.

The suspension is the result of (Name of Student)'s involvement in (Description of Infraction).

If you have questions about this suspension, please call me at (Phone Number).

Sincerely,

Principal

Discipline Letter 8.12

PARENT(S), SUSPENSION (3)

Elementary or Secondary

(Date)

(Name)

(Address)

Dear (Name):

This is to notify you that your child, (Name of Student), has been suspended from (Name of School) School for the following period of time: (Date) through (Date).

The reason for this suspension is (Description of Infraction).

On (Date) at (Time), we require you to accompany (Name of Student) to school for a short conference. This conference is required before (Name of Student) can be reinstated.

If you have any questions regarding this matter, please call me at (Phone Number).

Sincerely,

Principal

9

Letters Acknowledging Complaints

Acknowledgments should be brief and specific. One simply notes receipt of the complaint and indicates an intention to respond to the complaint as soon as further information is available.

Either written or verbal complaints may be received. The first obligation is to thank the individual for bringing the issue to the principal's attention. Copies of the letter written in response to the complaint should be maintained in appropriate files because complaints may not be easily resolved.

Letters acknowledging complaints may include the following:

Written or verbal complaints should be responded to with letters.

Concerns about book assignments may call for a letter of acknowledgment.

Continuing concerns about their children's education can necessitate letters to parents.

Letter Acknowledging Complaint 9.1

WRITTEN COMPLAINT

Elementary or Secondary

(Date)

(Address)

Dear (Name):

I want you to know that I received your letter dated (Date) concerning (Concern). I appreciate the opportunity to respond to your concern. I will look into the situation and contact you once I have more information.

Sincerely,

Principal

Letter Acknowledging Complaint 9.2

TELEPHONE COMPLAINT

Elementary or Secondary

(Date)

(Address)

Dear (Name):

This is to acknowledge your telephone call of (Date). I appreciate your bringing this issue to my attention. We have begun to inquire about the situation. When we have further information, we will call you.

If you have further concerns, please call us at (Phone Number) or send an e-mail message to (Name) at (E-mail Address).

Sincerely,

Principal

Letter Acknowledging Complaint 9.3

BOOK COMPLAINT

Elementary or Secondary

(Date)

(Address)

Dear (Name):

This is to acknowledge receipt of your letter about the (Concern) that your (Son/ Daughter) has been using (Book) in (His/Her) class.

I understand that you are concerned about (Concern).

Your (Son/Daughter) is excused from reading (Book). (Teacher Name) has been asked to provide (Name of Student) with another story on a different theme, one that you and (Name of Student) will not find objectionable.

We hope this addresses your concern.

Sincerely,

Principal

Letter Acknowledging Complaint 9.4

ONGOING COMPLAINT

Elementary

(Date)

(Address)

Dear (Name):

We received the message you sent yesterday, (Date). We have been in conversation about the perceived problem since (Date). We have met with you several times, exchanged messages, and talked with you by phone. We have also taken steps to ensure that (Describe Solution).

Your recent message indicates that you continue to have concerns. You mentioned that (Concern). Despite requests for (Name of Student) to immediately report such behavior to the adult in charge, we did not learn of the incident until (Name of Student) shared it with me on (Date). We do not tolerate such behavior, and when it occurs, we would like the opportunity to correct it right away. (Name of Student) can help by reporting any incident as soon as it occurs.

I would be pleased to meet with you if that would be helpful.

Sincerely,

Principal

10

Recommendation Letters

Letters of recommendation are written on behalf of individuals you know. The letters should be factual, noting specific skills or abilities of the individual. The focus should be on the individual's accomplishments in relation to the intention of the letter. Letters of recommendation and letters of reference are not synonymous. The letter of recommendation is written to advocate for an individual. The letter of reference documents an individual's employment or enrollment.

A principal has many opportunities to write letters of recommendation such as the following:

Teachers, student teachers, and staff members may request letters of recommendation when they apply for jobs.

Letters may also be written in support of teachers who are nominees for awards.

Students may request letters of recommendation when they seek employment and admission to colleges and universities.

Recommendation Letter 10.1

TEACHER JOB APPLICATION (1)

Elementary or Secondary

(Date)

(Name)

(Address)

Dear (Name):

(Name) has asked me to write a letter of recommendation on (His/Her) behalf. I am happy to do so. (Name) began (His/Her) teaching career at (Name of School) School in (Year). (He/She) has worked here for (Number) years. Presently, (Name) is the chairperson of the (Name of Department) Department working with (Number) other department teachers.

(Name) is an outstanding professional who works hard to make the (Name of Department) Department a model of excellence. (He/She) works well with teachers, students, parents, and administrators. Everyone appreciates (His/Her) knowledge and expertise in education.

(Name) is a leader who brings new and creative projects to the department. (Name of School) School has been fortunate to have a person of (Name)'s qualities working at the school.

I have no doubt that (Name) will continue to be an excellent educator. I highly recommend (Name) for the (Position) position at your school.

If I can supply any further information in support of (Name)'s application, please let me know.

Sincerely,

Principal

Recommendation Letter 10.2

TEACHER JOB APPLICATION (2)

Secondary

(Date)

To Whom It May Concern:

This is a letter of recommendation for (Name). (Name) taught in the (Department) at (Name of School) High School for the past (Number) years. I have found (Name) to be a student-centered teacher. Students ask to be in (His/Her) classes because they find the subject matter interesting and (Name) entertaining. Also, it is apparent (Name) has an excellent rapport with students; that is another reason students want to be in (His/Her) classes.

In addition to (His/Her) effective teaching skills, (Name) gives of (Himself/Herself) outside the classroom. (He/She) sponsors the (Name of Club) Club. With (His/Her) group, (Name) is well organized and works hard to ensure that students have a successful experience.

In conclusion, (Name) has been a very successful teacher at (Name of School), and (He/She) comes with my highest recommendation.

Sincerely,

Principal

Recommendation Letter 10.3

TEACHER JOB APPLICATION (3)

Elementary or Secondary

(Date)

(Name)

(Address)

Dear (Name):

I am writing this letter in support of (Name)'s application for the (Position) position at (Name of School) School.

I have had the opportunity to observe (Name)'s work during the (Number) years while (She/He) taught at (Name of School) School.

(Name) has excellent rapport with students. (Name)'s teaching is challenging and exciting for students. I'm certain (He/She) has copies of (His/Her) evaluations from (Number) years at (Name of School) School that document (His/Her) consistent, excellent teaching.

We are exceptionally sorry that (Name) is moving to (City, State). (He/She) will be truly missed here. I highly recommend (Name) for the (Position) position. If I can answer any questions you might have, please call me at (Phone Number).

Sincerely,

Principal

Recommendation Letter 10.4

STUDENT TEACHER JOB APPLICATION (1)

Elementary or Secondary

(Date)

(Name)

(Address)

Dear (Name):

I am pleased to recommend (Name) for a teaching position in the (Name of School District) School District. (Name) has exceptional skill and ability.

During the (Season) of the (Year) academic year, (Name) was a student teacher at (Name of School). (He/She) taught (Subject) to (Grade) students. (Name) was highly regarded by (His/Her) cooperating teacher. (He/She) worked well with all levels of ability and found ways to challenge all students.

(Name) has tremendous enthusiasm for teaching. Students enjoy (His/Her) classes and work hard to meet (His/Her) expectations. Students were actively involved in (Name)'s classes.

I highly recommend (Name) for the teaching position in your school district. (He/She) will be an excellent addition to your staff.

Sincerely,

Principal

Recommendation Letter 10.5

STUDENT TEACHER JOB APPLICATION (2)

Secondary

(Date)

To Whom It May Concern:

This is a letter of reference for (Name), who student taught at (Name of School) High School from (Year) to (Year). (Name)'s main responsibilities have been with (Subject) and (Subject).

(Name) has done an excellent job with (His/Her) student teaching assignment. (Name) is talented.

In addition, (Name) is dependable, and (He/She) is a hard worker. (Name)'s cooperating teacher, (Name), describes (Name) as highly motivated and effective.

It has been a pleasure to have (Name) student teach at (Name of School) High School this semester. If I can supply any further information in support of (Name)'s application, please let me know.

Sincerely,

Principal

Recommendation Letter 10.6

STAFF JOB APPLICATION

Elementary or Secondary

(Date)

(Name)

(Address)

Dear (Name):

(Name) has asked that I write a letter in support of (His/Her) application for the position of (Position). I am pleased to write on (Name)'s behalf.

(Name) was employed as a (Position) at (Name of School) School for (Number) years. During that time, (He/She) worked under the supervision of (Name) to organize materials for (Subject). In addition, (He/She) taught (Subject) to small groups of students. (He/She) did an outstanding job. (Name) had excellent rapport with students as well as staff. All staff members respected (Her/Him).

(Name) will be an asset to your school as well as to the school system.

If I can supply any further information in support of (His/Her) application, please let me know.

Sincerely,

Principal

Recommendation Letter 10.7

EDUCATOR AWARD NOMINATION

Elementary or Secondary

(Date)

To The Selection Committee:

Please accept this nomination of (Name) for the (Name of Award) Award. (Name) has taught at (Name of School) for (Number) years. (Name) has been a tremendous positive influence for the students of our school. Throughout (His/Her) career, (Name) has been recognized as an outstanding educator.

(Name) is highly regarded by all our teachers. (He/She) is dedicated, thoughtful, and on the cutting edge of the (Course) field. (Name) is frequently called on to make presentations at professional meetings because of (Name)'s expertise. These presentations are represented in the file provided in support of this nomination. (Name)'s leadership in education is clearly demonstrated through (His/Her) career.

It is truly an honor to nominate (Name) for the (Name of Award) Award. (Name) is most deserving of this honor.

Sincerely,

Principal

Recommendation Letter 10.8

PROFESSIONAL AWARD

Elementary or Secondary

(Date)

(Name)

(Address)

Dear (Name):

I recommend (Name) for the (Name of Award) Award presented by (Presenters).

I have known (Name) for the past (Number) years. During that time, (Name) has held the positions of (Position) and of (Position). (Name)'s responsibilities included (Responsibility) and (Responsibility).

(Name) is a strong leader who has unique abilities to mobilize staff, students, parents, and the community to work together to achieve the school's goals. Under the leadership of (Name), the school has accomplished the following:

(List Accomplishments)

(Name) is an outstanding (Position), who is an excellent candidate for the (Name of Award) Award. If I can supply any further information in support of (Name)'s nomination, please let me know.

Sincerely,

Principal

Recommendation Letter 10.9

STUDENT JOB APPLICATION

Secondary

(Date)

(Name)

(Address)

Dear (Name):

I am pleased to recommend (Name) as an excellent candidate for the (Position) position. (Name) has been a student at our school for the past (Number) years, during which time I have known (Him/Her) personally.

(Name) has many characteristics that make (Him/Her) an outstanding candidate for the (Position) position. (Name) is intelligent and dependable. (He/She) gets along well with others and is exceptionally hardworking. (Name) will be very successful at the (Position) position.

Sincerely,

Principal

Recommendation Letter 10.10

STUDENT ADMISSION

Secondary

(Date)

(Name)

(Address)

Dear (Name):

It is my pleasure to recommend (Name) for admission to (Name of University) University. (Name) is an outstanding student. (His/Her) academic record is excellent. (Name)'s achievements are noteworthy.

(Name) was a member of (Organization #1) for (Number) years, (Organization #2) for (Number) years, and (Organization #3) for (Number) years.

I recommend (Name) without reservation. If I can provide further information, please let me know.

Sincerely,

Principal

11

Job Application Letter

Occasionally, a principal may apply for a new position. A cover letter accompanied by a resume and a list of potential references are typically sent as an application. Following is an example of a letter used in an application for a position.

Application Letter 11.1

JOB APPLICATION

Elementary or Secondary

(Date)

(Name)

(Address)

Dear (Name):

I would like to be given consideration for the (Position) position announced in the (Journal/Paper). I am currently (Position) at (Name of School) School. I have held this position for (Number) years. Prior to this, I was a (Position) at (Name of School) School for (Number) years. I have had additional experience as a (Position), (Position), and (Position).

I hold a (Name of Degree) degree in (Subject) from (Name of University) University and a (Name of Degree) degree from (Name of University) University. My specialty areas are (Subject) and (Subject). I have had special training in (Subject) and (Subject), which are specific to the requirements stated in the position announcement.

I have included a copy of my resume with this letter. I have also included a list of individuals you might want to contact as references. I have an electronic portfolio that you can review at (Web address).

If I can provide any further information in support of my application, please call me at (Phone Number) (days) or (Phone Number) (evenings) or e-mail me at (E-mail address). Thank you for your consideration of this application. I look forward to hearing from you.

Sincerely,

Principal

Enclosure:

12

Special Events Letters

School events are announced through letters and invitations. Special events are important opportunities for building strong parent and community relationships. Invitations should be positive and encouraging because high attendance is a goal. The invitations should provide the important details about the event and sufficient description of the activity to elicit participation.

Invitations to *parents or guardians* might include the following:

Open Houses

Parent–teacher conferences

Special weeks at school

Parent workshops

Special meetings

Fundraising meetings and activities

Special Event Letter 12.1

OPEN HOUSE (1)

Elementary or Secondary

(Date)

(Name)

(Address)

Dear (Name):

Open House for families and students will be held (Day of the Week), (Date), at (Time). We hope you will be able to attend. You will be able to visit classes, see demonstrations, and tour the school. We will start with a brief informational presentation at (Time) in (Room at School).

Students will be available to answer questions. Refreshments will be served in the school cafeteria at (Time).

We look forward to seeing you soon.

Sincerely,

Principal

Special Event Letter 12.2

OPEN HOUSE (2)

Elementary or Secondary

(Date)

(Name)

(Address)

Dear (Name):

The (Name of School) School Open House will be held on (Day of the Week), (Date), from (Time) to (Time). You are also invited to meet with the Parent–Teacher Association from (Time) to (Time) in the (Room of School).

You will be able to visit the students' classrooms, view the displays of student work, visit with other parents, and visit with the teachers. Refreshments will be available in the (Room).

We look forward to seeing you on (Date).

Sincerely,

Principal

Special Event Letter 12.3

PARENT–TEACHER CONFERENCE (1)

Secondary

(Date)

(Name)

(Address)

Dear (Name):

Parent–teacher conferences for second semester will be from (Time) to (Time), (Date) and (Date). Each teacher is limited to conferences of no longer than seven minutes. It may not be possible for teachers to have conferences with every parent in the time allotted.

A schedule and an appointment form have been provided to help you identify the teachers you want to see. Please ask your son or daughter to fill in the schedule form with the subjects he or she is taking and the names of the teachers.

Time labels for each teacher will be posted in the (Room Number) by (Time) on the day of the conferences (one hour before the first scheduled conference time). To arrange for a teacher conference, remove one label for each teacher you wish to see and place it on your appointment form.

If all of the time labels for a specific teacher have been taken, that teacher will not be able to see you on conference night. You will need to call (School Office) to set up a different conference time to meet with that teacher.

School staff will be available to help arrange your conferences. Please do not hesitate to ask for help.

Sincerely,

Principal

Special Event Letter 12.4

PARENT–TEACHER CONFERENCE (2)

Elementary or Secondary

(Date)

(Name)

(Address)

Dear (Name):

Parent–teacher conferences will be held on (Day of Week), (Date) from (Time) P.M. to (Time) P.M. and on (Day of the Week), (Date) from (Time) A.M. to (Time) A.M. in the (Room at School). The conferences provide an opportunity for you to meet with teachers to discuss student progress. Conference times with individual teachers will be approximately 15 minutes long to allow teachers to visit with as many people as possible.

This is an excellent opportunity for you to visit with teachers about your child's progress during the first grading period. If you cannot attend a conference on these dates, please call (Phone Number) to arrange an alternate time.

We look forward to your participation.

Sincerely,

Principal

Special Event Letter 12.5

SPECIAL WEEK

Elementary

(Date)

(Name)

(Address)

Dear (Name):

On (Day of the Week), (Date), and (Day of the Week) at (Time), we will be celebrating (Name of Week) Week.

On (Date), we are asking all parents to join us for (Meal) at (Time) and on (Date), to join us for (Event). We would like to have you come and join us at (Time). After both events, we are going to read books to students, and the students would love to have you read to them or share the story time.

If you are able to come on either of these two dates and then stay to read, please call (Phone Number).

We hope to see you soon.

Sincerely,

Principal

Special Event Letter 12.6

WORKSHOP

Elementary

(Date)

(Name)

(Address)

Dear (Name):

You are invited to a special Parent Workshop on (Day of the Week), (Date), from (Time) to (Time). The speaker will be (Name) and the topic will be (Subject). The workshop will introduce activities you can use at home with your child as well as information about your child's needs at this age. You will also have the opportunity to visit with other parents.

Refreshments will be served.

We hope you will be able to attend this special workshop.

Sincerely,

Principal

Special Event Letter 12.7

PLANNING MEETING

Elementary or Secondary

(Date)

(Name)

(Address)

Dear (Name):

You are invited to attend our school district's strategic planning session on (Subject) on (Date) from (Time) to (Time) in the (Name of School) school auditorium. The session leader will be (Name).

The session will begin with a presentation to the whole group followed by small group meetings.

We hope you will be able to participate in this important meeting. If you have any questions, please call me at (Phone Number).

Sincerely,

Principal

Special Event Letter 12.8

MEETING

Elementary or Secondary

(Date)

(Name)

(Address)

Dear (Name):

The next meeting of the (Name of Council) Council will be at (Time) on (Date) in (Room Number). A tentative agenda for the meeting is enclosed. We expect (Name), (Name), and (Name) to attend.

As you know, the (Name of Council) Council is the (Description) for the school. The purpose of the meeting is to improve achievement and learning opportunities for all students.

We look forward to your participation.

Sincerely,

Principal

Special Event Letter 12.9

FUNDRAISING PLANNING

Elementary

(Date)

(Name)

(Address)

Dear (Name):

The Playground Project has had a successful beginning to its fundraising campaign. Currently, our fundraising efforts have totaled approximately (Dollar Amount).

As the committee considered projects for next year, they decided that more ideas and input are needed. We hope we can count on you for support and participation.

A planning meeting has been scheduled for (Date) in Room (Room Number) at the (Name of School) School. We hope you will be able to attend.

Sincerely,

Principal

Special Event Letter 12.10

BUSINESS DONATION FOR FUNDRAISING

Elementary

(Date)

(Name)

(Address)

Dear (Name):

The Parent–Teacher Organization at (Name of School) School has organized a fundraising drive for new playground equipment. We have two activities planned and hope your business will be able to make a donation. On (Date), we will hold a carnival and we would like to have door prizes. We will also hold a raffle of larger items. Raffle ticket sales will begin on (Date) with winners selected on (Date) at (Event).

Please consider donating an item that could be used as either a raffle item or a door prize. We will call you next week to discuss a possible donation. All donations will be collected by (Date).

Thank you for considering this request. If you have any questions, please call me at (Phone Number).

Sincerely,

Principal

Special Event Letter 12.11

PARENT(S), MAGAZINE DRIVE

Elementary or Secondary

(Date)

(Name)

(Address)

Dear Parents and Guardians,

The school magazine drive concluded on Friday, (Date). This was an extremely successful event this year. Of the (Number) families in our school, (Number/%) of the families were able to participate. This high participation resulted in a profit of (Dollar Amount) that will be distributed to the activities identified by the parents group.

Thank you for your support of this fundraiser! Thanks, especially, to the parents group and volunteers who organized and managed the fundraiser.

The students are, once again, the beneficiaries of our collaborative efforts!

Sincerely,

Principal

Special Event Letter 12.12

PARENT(S), FUNDRAISING PARTICIPATION (1)

Elementary or Secondary

(Date)

(Name)

(Address)

Dear Parents and Guardians,

Please keep in mind the variety of fundraising efforts initiated by our school parents and booster organizations. These activities provide opportunities for you to contribute to the support of the broad array of enrichment, recreation, and athletic programs for the students.

Keep in mind that there will be a magazine sale during (Dates). You might want to plan your magazine purchases or renewals during this time.

We will have a carnival on (Date). Please reserve this date. The children really enjoy this event. You may want to volunteer to assist at one of the activities for an hour. The contact person is (Name) and (His/Her) telephone number is (Telephone Number), and (His/Her) e-mail address is (E-mail Address).

We have been selling SCRIP through the parents group for the past five years. This has been an extremely successful fundraiser. SCRIP is available from the area grocery stores, bookstores, department stores, nurseries, gasoline stations, video stores, and restaurants. A complete listing of available SCRIP can be found at the SCRIP Web site (Web Address). Please contact (Name, Telephone Number, E-mail Address) with your questions. You can purchase SCRIP after school in room (Room Number) every school day. Remember, a percentage of each purchase is returned to the parents group for our students' programs.

The annual Pizza Feed–School in Review movie night will be held on (Date). This is an exciting event since it is the first time the students get to see the videos taken of them throughout the year in their various school activities. We hope you'll be able to attend this and all the other activities that support our students and build the strength of our school community!

Sincerely,

Principal

Special Event Letter 12.13

PARENT(S), FUNDRAISING PARTICIPATION (2)

Elementary

HOLIDAY GREETINGS!

During past years, the parent group at (Name of School) has been responsible for making many special purchases for the (Description). These are usually things that are not included in the (Type of Budget) budget.

Without parent support of fundraisers, children would not have many of the special things that make their school day a fun learning experience.

Work is already in progress for the (Name of Fundraiser). This is our largest fundraiser for the year, and we need your help. When you see a request for volunteers, please sign up. This is a great way to get to know other families and show your child that good things happen when we all work together.

Take a look at the items listed below and see how past contributions have helped make (Name of School) a terrific place for kids.

Thank you and Happy Holidays from the (Name of School)!

Outdoor Items	*Shared Items*	*Miscellaneous Items*
Tricycles	Computers	Field trips
Playhouse	Musical instruments	Teacher appreciation
Sand and sand toys	Hardcover books	Telephones in all rooms
	Balance beam	

Special Event Letter 12.14

PARENT(S), FUNDRAISING PARTICIPATION (3)

Elementary

Subject: The Importance of the (Name of School) Fund and How It Supports Our School

Each year, the (Name of School) Parent–Teacher Organization (PTO) supports our school with additional funds. The PTO has made the following contributions:

(List Contributions)

This year, the PTO will be contributing funds to special events. The PTO also sponsors teacher recognitions and many other special projects throughout the year.

The (Name of School) Fund was started in (Year) as our only source of fundraising (no door-to-door sales). We have estimated that if each family could contribute $25, we would raise approximately $10,000. The fund is clearly the easiest way to raise this amount of money with only two volunteers chairing the event. If you have ever been involved in a fundraiser, you know that it requires a lot of time and volunteers.

Each grade level will be given an equal amount of money. The PTO will be gathering ideas and voting on projects at scheduled PTO meetings. All PTO expenditures are discussed and voted on at the regular PTO meetings.

Any contribution you can make to the fund will be appreciated!

If you have any questions or suggestions, please contact me.

Sincerely,

Principal

Special Event Letter 12.15

PARENT(S), INVITATION
KINDERGARTEN ROUND-UP

Elementary

Date

Name

Address

City, State Zip

Dear Parents and Guardians:

Kindergarten Round-Up will be held (Date) at (Time) in (Room Number) in (Building). Any child who has reached the age of (Age) by (Date) will be eligible to attend Kindergarten in the fall of (Year).

Registration forms will be mailed (Date). You can pick up forms in room (Number) of the (Name Building). Please bring these completed forms to the Roundup. You will also be required to bring a copy of the child's Certificate of Live Birth. This is the official certificate that is available from the Bureau of Vital Statistics.

If you have any questions about Kindergarten Roundyup, please e-mail (Name) at (E-mail Address) or phone (Him/Her) at (Telephone Number).

We look forward to seeing you (Day), (Date), at (Time).

Sincerely,

Principal

13

Opening Comments for Special Events

Although not strictly letters, the examples given in this chapter can certainly be time savers for busy principals. As a principal, you have many speaking opportunities. School programs, awards and honors ceremonies, civic activities, parent meetings, and celebrations are some of the events that provide speaking opportunities. As you prepare for these events, consider the following issues:

Who is the audience? (Obviously, we talk differently to children than to adults.)

How will I elicit the interest of the audience?

How will I make my presentation memorable for the audience?

What are the main ideas I want to convey to the audience?

How much time is available for the presentation?

Examples of opening comments you may be asked to provide can include the following:

Open Houses

Award ceremonies

Special ceremonies

Conferences

Nominating candidates for offices

Opening 13.1

OPEN HOUSE

Elementary

Welcome to the (Name of School) Open House. I am (Name), principal of (Name of School). I am pleased that you are here tonight. We have a long tradition of providing a fine educational setting for teaching and learning.

As you know, our school mission is (Mission).

We must work together to achieve that mission. We know that today's children will face challenges and opportunities we cannot even imagine this afternoon. As partners in their education, we must prepare them for their exciting future.

Our schedule for this evening is (Schedule).

Thank you for coming to the Open House. Your support and interest are essential to the children's positive school experiences.

Opening 13.2

AWARD CEREMONY (1)

Elementary or Secondary

Good Evening! This is a great opportunity to recognize the accomplishments of our students.

The (Name of Award) is presented to an outstanding individual who (Criteria for Award).

Tonight we recognize this individual's accomplishment (State the individual's accomplishment).

A committee of judges consisting of (Names and Positions) determined the winner of this award.

The criteria used in the selection were (Criteria).

The winner is (Name).

(Present the award and shake hands with the winner. Ask the person to make a few remarks.)

Opening 13.3

AWARD CEREMONY (2)

Elementary or Secondary

Good Evening. The (Name of Award) Award is presented to an outstanding individual who has provided exceptional service to education. Tonight, we are here to recognize the accomplishments of an outstanding individual and present the (Name of Award) Award.

The selection committee for this award consisted of representatives from the state department of education, the school board, the city parks and recreation department, and the YMCA. The pool of candidates was outstanding. Selecting a winner was clearly a challenge.

To be a candidate for this award, the person must be an active member of educational organizations, must have been involved in education for five or more years, and must be currently active in a specific education project.

The winner of the (Name of Award) Award is (Name). Among (Name)'s activities are the following: (List activities)

-

-

-

It is a pleasure to present this award to (Name).

Opening 13.4

SPECIAL CEREMONY

Elementary or Secondary

Thank you for coming to this special ceremony to dedicate and name our new (Building/Center) in honor of (Name). (Name) was the (Position) from (Year) to (Year). During (Name)'s tenure in this position, (He/She) accomplished the following: (Accomplishment), (Accomplishment), (Accomplishment), and (Accomplishment). The naming of the (Building/Center) in honor of (Name) is especially appropriate because (Name) had a special interest in (Name of School). This reflects (Name)'s commitment to this aspect of education. Many of you have contributed in special ways to make the (Building/Center) possible. Thank you again for your efforts. It's great to see what we are able to accomplish when we set goals for ourselves.

We are particularly pleased that (Name) is here today, accompanied by (His/Her) family members. We are pleased to be able to enjoy this special event with them. We hope (Name) will share a few comments with us, too.

Opening 13.5

INTRODUCING CONFERENCE SPEAKER

Elementary or Secondary

Good afternoon. It is a pleasure to introduce (Name), our conference speaker, the Director of (Department). As we begin this new era, (Name)'s topic, (Name of Topic), is especially timely.

This is how the demographics of our country have changed: (Comparative Demographics of the United States).

This is how the demographics of our community have changed: (Comparative Demographics of the Community).

Today, our keynote speaker, (Name), will share (Description). In addition to (Name)'s important role with (Organization), (Name) is the (Description). (Name) earned (His/Her) bachelor's degree in (Department/Specialty) from the University of (Name of University), and (He/She) earned a master's degree from (Name of University) in (Department/Specialty). We are fortunate to have (Name) as our speaker today, and I am pleased to present (Name) to you.

Opening 13.6

CONFERENCE

Elementary or Secondary

Good afternoon! Welcome to the (Number) Annual (Name of Conference) Conference sponsored by the (Name of Sponsor). During the past (Number) years, this conference has addressed the issue of (Subject of Conference). Our efforts have resulted in (Accomplishments). For these reasons, I am proud to be a member of the organization, and it gives me great pleasure to welcome you here.

Today, more than (Number) are in attendance at this conference where we will address the critical issue of (Subject). As we begin a new era, we want to (Goals for the Future).

Again, welcome to the (Number) Annual (Name of Conference) Conference. We hope it will be an outstanding experience for you.

Opening 13.7

NOMINATION

Elementary or Secondary

I am pleased to nominate (Name) for the office of (Position) of the (Name of Organization). This position requires a dedicated individual who can (Qualifications). The person must be able to work effectively with the members, including (Qualification), (Qualification), and (Qualification). (Name) has served as (Position) for (Number) years. (Name) has also been an active contributor to (Organization), (Organization), and (Organization). (Name) has a commitment to this organization as evidenced by (His/Her) work as (Position), (Position), and (Position) during the past (Number) years.

Because of (Name)'s qualifications, I am confident that coupled with (His/Her) experiences and fine people skills, (Name) will be excellent in the position of (Position).

Thank you for the opportunity to present this nomination.

**CORWIN
PRESS**

The Corwin Press logo—a raven striding across an open book—represents the union of courage and learning. Corwin Press is committed to improving education for all learners by publishing books and other professional development resources for those serving the field of PreK–12 education. By providing practical, hands-on materials, Corwin Press continues to carry out the promise of its motto: **"Helping Educators Do Their Work Better."**